The Noble Grapes
and the Great Wines
of France

The wrapper and endpapers are reproduced from a photograph by Percy Hennell of part of a private cellar in an English country house and demonstrate the different shapes and sizes of French wine bottles.

Bottles 1, 2, 3, and 4 are all CLARET bottles; (1) is a jeroboam or double magnum of Château Mouton d'Armailhac 1934; (2) is a magnum, or two bottles, of Château Léoville Poyferré 1924; (3) is the rarely found tregnum or three bottles (in Scotland sometimes called a 'tappit hen') of Château Ausone 1933; (4) is a half-bottle of Château Margaux 1934. (5) is a bottle of fine and very old BURGUNDY from a tiny vineyard in Aloxe Corton, near Beaune – this shape of bottle is also used for CHAMPAGNE and most of the wines of ANJOU. (6) is a SAUTERNES from the famous Château d'Yquem – most, but not all, BRANDY is bottled in a similar shaped bottle; the bottle used as a candle-holder (7) is an English eighteenth-century wine bottle holding about a pint (the general use then of this smaller kind of bottle explains, to some extent, the 'five bottle man' of those days); (8) is a tasting glass in general use throughout France, and (9) is a Burgundian silver tasting cup, a Tastevin.

A bottle of ALSACE is not shown, but corresponds to the normal German Hock or Moselle bottle.

The Noble
GRAPES
and the Great
WINES
of France

By ANDRÉ L. SIMON

WITH 24 COLOUR PHOTOGRAPHS BY PERCY HENNELL
AND EIGHT MAPS AND DECORATIONS BY
ASGEIR SCOTT

OCTOPUS BOOKS

This edition published by arrangement with
McGraw-Hill Book Company Inc.
330 West 42nd Street, New York City 36

by Octopus Books Limited
59 Grosvenor Street,
London W 1

© George Rainbird Ltd

Library of Congress Catalog Card No: 72/86098

Produced by Mandarin Publishers Limited
77a Marble Road, North Point, Hong Kong
and printed in Hong Kong

Contents

The Colour Plates

THE GRAPES APPEAR ON THE PAGE IN THEIR ACTUAL SIZE

vii

The Maps
(At end of book)

Introduction

ONE MIGHT WELL ask if there is any need for another book about French wines, and should there be such a need, one might well ask if I can possibly have anything new to say. I have not, but it does not matter. This book is entirely different from any of the sixty-odd wine books which I have written during the past fifty years. It is a book unlike all the books which have been published so far about the wines of France. Why? Because it is the first book which gives a true picture of some of the wines made from different sorts of grapes. It is the first time in the history of the wine trade and of the book trade that you will be able to see the exact size, shape and colour of the Cabernets, Pinots and other grapes, as well as the exact colour of the wines made from each of the main varieties of grapes.

There are no words in English, French or any other language capable of conveying to a reader's mind the differences existing in the shades of 'gold' of the wines of Bordeaux, Burgundy and Alsace, wines which we call 'white' although there has never been a really white wine any more than a truly white grape.

Why has it never been done before? First of all because it could not be done before the recent development in the art – it is more than skill – of colour photography, of which I believe Percy Hennell to be the greatest exponent. In the second place, because to transfer his colours to paper without loss of quality is a very costly business, and it has not been easy to find a publisher, willing, able, and courageous enough to undertake such a publication which is in itself a major operation.

Percy Hennell's beautiful pictures of grapes and their wines make this a most desirable book for all wine-lovers to possess, as well as a valuable book of reference for wine-merchants. As regards the text, I can claim for it, without false modesty, (a) that facts and figures are as reliable as possible[1]; and (b) that judgements which are a matter of personal opinion are based upon experience gained during the sixty consecutive years during which I have drunk wine daily.

Grapes grow and wine is made almost everywhere in France, and fully a third of the 4,500 million gallons of wine which flow from all the world's vineyards every year is French wine. Most of it, probably 90%, is *ordinaire* or plain wine, which is either drunk where it is made and within a year, or else it is distilled when three or six months old. The other 10%, a small proportion of the whole, but on an average some 150 million gallons of better wines, is made up of a very large variety of wines, from light and charming 'little' wines, to the world-famous 'great' wines of Bordeaux and Burgundy. I contend that many of these 'little' wines may and often do deserve to be called 'grand' wines, just as many a friend may be and often is a grand fellow who never was a great man. Few are alive today who have enjoyed more or better wines than I have in the course of a long and well-wined life, and I can truthfully say that I remember the many friendly, charming and helpful 'little' wines as gratefully as the rarer and dearer greater ones.

All French 'quality wines' are now known, in France, as AC wines, or *Appellations contrôlées* wines, and some of our readers may welcome a little information about these *Appellations contrôlées*.

After the disastrous visitation of the American vine louse, the *Phylloxera vastatrix*, during the latter part of the nineteenth century, the vineyards of France were all but destroyed and before they could be replanted there was an acute shortage of wine: it led, unfortunately, not only to high prices but to many fraudulent practices which the existing laws, intended to protect the public from misdescriptions, could not check. It is not for the seller to prove that his goods are what he calls them but for the buyer to prove that they are not: it is easy enough for him to show that he has been given a cotton shirt which was invoiced as a silk one, but not nearly so easy to prove that he was given some Algerian wine which had been sold to him as Burgundy. The first law to deal with the matter was that of the 1st August, 1905, since when a very large number of other decrees, laws and ordinances have been published in the *Journal Officiel;* they have been recorded in *La protection des appellations d'origine des vins et eaux-de-vie et le Commerce des vins*[1], a large in-8 volume of 708 pages. There is, since the 16th July, 1947, an *Institut national des appellations d'origine des*

---

[1] Vineyards may change hands and may be renamed; some may go out of cultivation and other be replanted at any time.

vins et spiritueux, and this official body is responsible for the granting or refu
sing to all quality wines throughout France their own distinctive AC or *Appellation contrôlée*.

In writing the Introduction to our book I am aware that the book itself is but
an introduction to the pleasures and mysteries of wine. It could happen, and I
hope it will, that many readers will be tempted to visit the homes of these great
and little wines of my native land. They will be very welcome at the vast majority of vineyards, large and small; they will be given to taste the wine of two or
three years perhaps, and they will not be asked to buy. It is advisable to obtain
an introduction beforehand, preferably through a wine merchant, failing which
one should call upon the Conseil Interprofessionnel du Vin de Bordeaux,
1 Cours du 30 Juillet, Bordeaux; or the Conseil Interprofessionnel du Vin de
Champagne, 23 rue Henri Martin, Epernay, when in Champagne; or the local
Syndicats d'Initiative elsewhere.

May this book bear witness to my affection and gratitude for the Grand Wines
of my native land, be they little or great.

A. L. S.

Published by *La Journée Vinicole*. Montpellier. 1949.

Acknowledgments

A list of some of our French friends to whom we are indebted for the help they gave Percy Hennell at the vintage time when our photographs were taken: M. Georges Bouchard, Beaune (Bouchard Ainé, Fils & Cie); M. Georges Couvreur, Epernay (Maison De Venoge); M. Christian Cruse, Bordeaux (Cruse, Fils, Frères & Cie); M. J. Dargent, Reims (Comité Interprofessionnel du Vin de Champagne); M. J. Deramond, Paris (Comité National de Propagande en faveur du Vin); M. A. Devletian, Paris (Institut National des Appellations d'Origine); M. René Dopff, Riquewihr (Dopff & Irion); M. Jean Dubois-Challon, Saint-Emilion (Château Ausone); M. Raymond Filioux, Cognac (J. Hennessy & Co.); M. Michel Jaboulet-Vercherre, Tain-L'Ermitage (S. A. H. Jaboulet-Vercherre); M. M. Marsay, Sauternes (Château d'Yquem); M. M. Monmousseau, Saint-Hilaire-Saint-Florent, près Saumur (Maison Bouvet-Ladubay); M. M. Valery Taulier, Tavel (Clos Canto Perdrix); M. Paul Tijon, Beaulieu-sur-Layon (Domaine de la Soncherie).

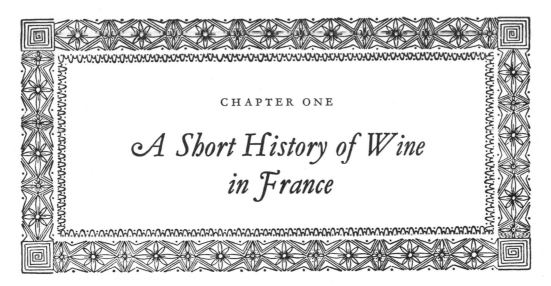

CHAPTER ONE

A Short History of Wine
in France

THERE WERE VINES growing wild and free in many parts of the land which we now know as France long before there were Frenchmen or anybody else to eat grapes or to make wine. Fossils which modern palaeontology ascribes to the early stages of the crust formation of the earth bear witness to it. When the Phoenicians laid the foundations of Marseilles in 600 B.C., they had no need to bring cuttings of their own Eastern vines: they had only to prune, train and tend the native vines in order to get better grapes and to make wine. Centuries later, when flourishing vineyards and olive groves attracted the unwelcome barbarians from the North and the East, Marseilles appealed to Rome for help, and presently the people of Marseilles had no longer any cause to fear the inroads of barbarians, for Rome took over their hinterland altogether and made it into a Roman Province, known to this day as Provence. What Rome wanted from Marseilles as well as from Carthage, across the Mediterranean, was food, chiefly wheat, and not wine. Italy, with the exception of the northern plains and the Po Valley, is a mountainous and poor country, but grapes will grow and wine can be made where the soil is too poor for grain, root crops or pastures. Rome was always on the look-out for granaries overseas and outlets for the surplus wine of Italian vineyards, which is why Domitian ordered the uprooting of all transalpine vineyards in 92 A.D., when a poor harvest had caused much distress in Italy. Domitian's Edict was certainly aimed at the sunny lands of Provence where grain would surely grow in place of vines, grain which was so badly wanted in Italy, when it could be shipped from Marseilles so easily. Whatever vines were growing at the time on the steep slopes of the Jura and Vosges mountains, or in the faraway valleys of the Rhine and Marne, were most likely left alone; whatever wine they brought forth never reached Italy. Recently, when Roman galleys sunk outside the port of Marseilles nearly two thousand years ago were freed from the sand and slime which had sealed them and their contents so long, it was found that their cargo consisted entirely of great amphorae of Italian wine, proof that the Provence vineyards had ceased to exist at the time.

On the other hand, when Caesar forged ahead and completed the conquest of Gaul, the rivers were his easiest lines of communication across a land without any roads, and, for safety's sake, he cleared the river banks and the slopes of their valleys from forests in which the hostile population could hide and harass his advancing legions. His next move was to coax here and there the more amenable of the natives to plant a vineyard and to make wine, as the surest means of attaching them to the soil and making them his allies in its defence. And to this day there are still vineyards along the great rivers of France, Rhône, Loire, Saône, Marne and Seine claiming a Roman origin, although many of those very ancient vineyards have completely or almost disappeared. There are still, unknown to most Parisians, two "token" vineyards left on two of the seven hills of Paris, at Montmartre and Mont Valérien.

Caesar had nothing to do with Bordeaux. It was Crassus, with Caesar and Pompey as triumvir, in 60 B.C. who brought the *Pax Romana* to the Atlantic coast, but there were flourishing vineyards already there and their owners were not molested. We know how prosperous the Bordeaux vinelands were during the Gallo-Roman era, roughly speaking from 50 B.C. to 400 A.D., from memoirs and poems of that age, none better known than those of Ausonius, the Bordeaux-born son of a Roman Senator: he had a very brilliant career as a lawyer, consul, and governor in Italy, at Trier and in Asia Minor; he retired, wrote verse and eventually died at his villa just outside the walls of the old city of Saint Emilion, where stands today the famous Château Ausone.

With the successive waves of barbarians from the East who swamped the Gallo-Roman culture during the fifth century, viticulture must have suffered greatly, but it was saved by the Church. Clovis, who had captured Soissons in 486, and then Paris, was the first king of the Franks to be received into the Church by St Rémi, the Archbishop of Reims. St Rémi, according to tradition, gave Clovis a flask of wine which he had blessed so effectively that the King could and did drink out of it whenever in need of refreshment without the flask having to be refilled. St Rémi's will, which can still be read, provides more reliable evidence of the prelate's appreciation of wine, and of the antiquity of the

Champagne vineyards: there are in this will a number of bequests of vineyards, some of which had been planted by the Archbishop, whilst others had been given to him, in various parts of the Marne valley.

No evidence has so far come to light that any vineyards were planted in the valley of the Marne above Epernay and the Montagne de Reims before 210 A.D., when the Emperor Probus officially cancelled Domitian's Edict prohibiting the planting of vineyards beyond the Alps. According to tradition, the Roman legions were encamped at the time in the plain of Châlons-sur-Marne, without any fighting or anything else to do, and they were given the job of clearing the forests that covered the Montagne de Reims and to break up the ground so that vines could be planted, where they have been thriving ever since.

Saint Eloi, Bishop of Noyon, and Saint Ouen, Bishop of Rouen, were the advisers, in the seventh century, of good King Dagobert, who created the Duchy of Aquitaine, for his brother Caribert. In the eighth century, Charlemagne, Emperor of the West, gave his wholehearted protection to the Church and much encouragement to viticulture. During his long reign (771–814) many vineyards were planted in Burgundy and the Rhineland which were, during many centuries, among the most famous in the world for the excellence of their wines. It was also during the reign of Charlemagne that the Saracens, who had ruined many vineyards of Aquitaine, were driven out of France.

All through the Dark Ages – and after – when force was the only law and life was cheap, wine was made from the grapes of one vintage to be drunk within the ensuing twelve months, just as bread was made from the grain of one harvest to last until the next and no more. No wine can hope to be a great wine within a year, and no one bothers to make with particular care a wine that can never be great. Which is why the only great wines of France of long ago were some of the wines made by the mediaeval religious Orders: they had the land, the money, the knowledge, the labour, and above all the will to make the best possible wine to the greater glory of God, and to keep it safely until it had attained its optimum quality.

There is no more illustrious example of a monastic vineyard, in France, than the Clos de Vougeot, the largest as well as one of the finest of the vineyards of Burgundy. When some poor, uncultivated land in the valley of the little river Vouge was bequeathed to the nearby Abbey of Cîteaux, in 1110, some of the owners of small vineyards close by also gave them to the monks, who were able to buy, now and again, whenever the opportunity offered, more land or vineyards; eventually, in 1336, they were able to build a wall enclosing a splendid vineyard of some 125 acres, which remained their property until the French Revolution of 1789. Today, this vineyard has been divided among a large number of small owners, but most of the wall still stands, and the great

Celliers and Pressoir of the monks still bear witness to their industry and skill.

An event which had the most unexpected consequences as regards the wines of Bordeaux was the marriage of Eleanor of Aquitaine, only child of the last Duc d'Aquitaine, with Henri Plantagenet, Comte d'Anjou, in 1152. When Henri Plantagenet became King Henry II of England, in 1154, the people of all his own and his wife's possessions in France became subjects of the King of England, with the same duties, rights and privileges as his English-born subjects. This meant that during the next three hundred years the Bordeaux-born merchants could – and did – sell their wines in England as Englishmen, not foreigners. They had their own Company in London, the Vintners' Company, one of the twelve great Livery Companies, the liverymen of which elected then, as they do now, the Lord Mayors of London. This is how Sir Henry Picard, when Master of the Vintners' Company, was Lord Mayor of London, in 1335, and entertained at Vintners' Hall five Kings, Edward III, King of England and Duc d'Aquitaine; King John of France, who had been taken prisoner at the Battle of Poitiers and was at the time Edward's "guest" at the Savoy; David, King of Scotland; Hugh IV, King of Cyprus, and Waldemar, King of Denmark.

In France, at the time, difficulties of transport made it practically impossible to send wine from one province to the next; besides tolls and taxes, there were highwaymen that made it far too risky to be attempted. The people of Paris drank wines from the vineyards of the Seine and the Marne chiefly; some wines from Orléans and the Yonne, but never from faraway Bordeaux. To be given what amounted to a monopoly of the sale of table wines, in England, was for the *vignerons* and merchants of the Gironde a wonderful chance; it made the fortune of many of them, and it also made them all desperately loyal to the English Crown. In those days, when most of the water available was surface water and anything but safe to drink, everybody but the poorest in the land drank wine, and lots of it, at a penny per gallon, so that the demand for the wines of Bordeaux, in England, was very considerable indeed.

After the battle of Castillon, in 1453, when Talbot, whose name lives to this day in the wine of Château Talbot, one of the *Crus Classés du Médoc*, was killed, Bordeaux was lost to the English Crown, the people of Bordeaux ceased to have any claim to English citizenship, and their trade in England suffered a serious setback. In spite of this, however, the wines of Bordeaux were still in greater demand in London than in Paris, until the eighteenth century, when the Duc de Richelieu, a son of the great Cardinal de Richelieu's nephew, was Gouverneur de Guyenne et Gascogne.

During the reign of Louis XIV (1643–1715) there had been very keen competition between the wines of Burgundy and Champagne to gain the King's favour. There was only very little sparkling wine made in Champagne at the time. Most

Plate 1 André Simon in Ay vineyard in Champagne

Champagne wines were still, red, table wines, made from Pinot grapes and not unlike the lighter red wines of Burgundy. Sparkling Champagne, however, was something new and much more costly than the still wine, two perfectly good reasons why a court physician would recommend it to his royal master, who probably wanted to drink this new wine anyhow. The Burgundians were, of course, very cross with Fagon, Louis XIV's physician, for letting the King drink a wine, the only merit of which was to be a *"vin de débauche"* – a fast living wine, said they. The Champenois held a meeting at the Reims Ecole de Médecine on the 5th May, 1700, when they claimed that Champagne was not only the pleasantest of all wines to drink, but also the most wholesome; they supported this claim by producing a document proving that a native of Hautvillers, Pierre Piéton, who had never drunk any other wine but Champagne, had lived to the ripe age of 118. The challenge was immediately taken up by the Burgundians, who produced a native of Beaune, Baron de Villebertin, who had never tasted any other wine except Burgundy, and who had lived to be 120. They also claimed that the Pope and the King of Spain always drank Burgundy. The Champenois might have claimed that good King Henry IV, a Basque by birth, whose lips had first tasted Jurançon wine at his christening, had been so fond of Champagne when he had come to the throne and to Paris, that he called himself "Roi de France et de Navarre et Sire d'Ay". His first wife, Reine Margot, had apparently a thirst both rabelaisian and regal; in 1600, after their marriage had been annulled, she sent a messenger to the King with a written request for an exemption of taxes on 500 *tonneaux de vin pour sa bouche*. Henri refused and wrote across the preposterous demand: *c'est se déclarer ivrognesse en parchemin* – this is legally to proclaim herself a drunk.

It was during the reign of Henri IV (1593–1619) that Olivier de Serres was able, thanks to royal patronage and encouragement, to introduce improved methods of viticulture which were responsible for greater quantities of wine of better quality being produced in many parts of France, in the Médoc more especially. Olivier de Serres did much to reclaim large areas of unproductive marshland between the Gironde and the sea, and the prosperity of the Médoc at the time was due to him.

Up to the latter part of the seventeenth century, the Graves vineyards produced the Bordeaux wines which were the more popular in England and Scotland, but the Médoc took the lead from the beginning of the eighteenth century and never lost it. In 1723, for instance, two English wine-merchants were in Bordeaux for the vintage: Mr Bruneval, who sold wine to the Prince of Wales, and Mr Bennett, who was the wine-merchant of the prime minister, Sir Robert Walpole. One of Bruneval's letters, dated 16th October, 1723, from Bordeaux, may still be seen at Raynham Hall, in Norfolk, among the Townshend MSS. and

Plate 2 The flush of youth. The red wines of France when young are rich and brilliant as the wine in this glass, a glass suitable for almost any wine.

in it Bruneval placed Lafite, Latour, Margaux and Pontac [1] in a class by themselves, but adds "never in my life have I tasted the Château d'Issan as good as
this vintage".

By the middle of the eighteenth century, the principal growths of the Médoc
had already been "classed" or grouped, if not officially, as in 1855, at least effectively, by a scale of prices which was agreed to by the growers of the Médoc
and the merchants of Bordeaux. These were the agreed rates for the wines of the
1750 vintage, per *tonneau*, of approximately 252 (U.S.) gallons or 210 (U.K.)
imperial gallons.

> Premiers Crus: 2,400 Livres [2]
> Deuxièmes Crus: 2,100   ,,
> Troisièmes Crus: 1,400   ,,
> Quatrièmes Crus 850   ,,
> Cinquièmes Crus 500   ,,
> Vins ordinaires   160 to 300 Livres.

Louis XV was not a good king, but a gay one who made sparkling Champagne fashionable at court, and somewhat disreputable to the bourgeois mind
at the time, that is, during the latter part of the eighteenth century. Of far greater
importance to the prosperity of the vineyards of France during the reign of
Louis XV (1715–1774) was the great stimulus given to the export of wine overseas, chiefly to Scandinavia and Russia, and French settlements and colonies in
North America, Africa and India. This export trade benefited the *vignerons* and
merchants of Bordeaux far more than those of Burgundy or Champagne, who
had nothing like the same facilities of despatch and shipment. Strange to say, the
Intendants, the forerunners of today's *Préfets* of the Gironde, were not in the least
helpful: on the contrary, they prohibited the planting of new vineyards on a
number of occasions, when the vintage proved to be excellent, both as regards
the quality and the exceptionally large quantity of wines made. In 1723, the
Intendant Boucher went further and ordered that the vines of some Bordeaux
vineyards be uprooted. Montesquieu gallantly and successfully opposed him. As

---

[1]   The name of the owner of Château Haut-Brion. In London, during the seventeenth
century, Pontac was considered the best red Bordeaux. John Evelyn wrote on 13 July,
1683, that he had met Monsieur Pontac, 'the son of the famous Bordeaux President who
owns the excellent vineyards of Pontac and Haut-Brion, whence the best Bordeaux wines
come from.'

[2]   *Livres tournois*, not *Livres sterling*. There were 20 *sols* to the *livre*, and 12 *deniers* to
the *sol*, up to the French Revolution of 1789, when the old currency collapsed and was
eventually replaced by the metric system with the *Franc* of 100 *centimes* as the basic unit.
The *Livre tournois* corresponded roughly, in value, to 50 cents or 3s 6d of the present
U.S. and U.K. currencies.

a lawyer and the owner of a vineyard at Château de la Brède, where he was born, he protested against what he called an insufferable interference with the liberty of each man to put to whatever use he thought best whatever belonged to him. Ten years later, when another *Intendant*, Tourny, prohibited the planting of new vineyards and ordered the uprooting of some old ones, on the plea that there would soon be too much wine and not enough bread, Montesquieu once more protested and very sensibly remarked that the more wine there was the greater and the more profitable would be the sale of wine, adding that there would not be any likelihood of bread shortage if the *Intendant* removed or relaxed the iniquitous taxes that kept out of Bordeaux the wheat which nearby provinces, such as Languedoc, would be only too ready to sell. In 1717, Bordeaux exported 7,000 *tonneaux* of wine to French settlements in Africa, and 37,000 *tonneaux* fifty years later. The average production of the Gironde, during the reign of Louis XV was 200,000 *tonneaux*, of which 125,000 *tonneaux* were exported and 75,000 *tonneaux* consumed locally, the more important markets being:

from 2,000 to 6,000 *tonneaux* of the best red wines of the Médoc to England;

30,000 *tonneaux* of red and white wines, mostly white, to Holland and the Scandinavian countries;

30,000 *tonneaux* of the commoner red wines to the French colonies;

25,000 *tonneaux* of both red and white wines, mostly from the Graves de Bordeaux vineyards, to Paris and other parts of France.

The French Revolution and the wars of the Napoleonic period were not favourable to the making and maturing of fine wines. Napoleon is said to have been partial to Chambertin, but it is very doubtful whether he ever appreciated any of the fine wines of France; his chance of drinking any of them came when he was not so much too old as too much otherwise preoccupied. Except on rare ceremonious occasions, he bolted his food and wine, a very bad habit indeed which killed him in the end.

Napoleon's fiscal reform was less spectacular but of far more solid worth than the glory which crowned so many of his victories, at the cost of half the male population of the country. For over a hundred years, the value of the French franc was absolutely stable, and the prosperity which France enjoyed was due, to a very great extent, to the confidence which such stability encouraged both at home and abroad.

During the hundred years, from Waterloo to the First World War, more wealth was lavished upon the great vineyards of France than ever before. Some of the richest among the families of the old French nobility and some of the more famous among the international bankers, as well as large landowners and merchant-princes whose wealth dated from the Revolution or the Napoleonic wars, were, as their descendants are today, equally proud to own some of the finest vineyards of France, and they never spared any expense to make and mature wines of superlative quality.

There were, in all probability, more and finer wines made in France from 1830 to 1880 than had ever been made before from all the vineyards of the world. Wines were so good and there was so much of them during that blessed half century that they could be, or often had to be, kept; they were thus given a chance to show how great they could be.

And then came that greatest of all calamities, which killed outright most of the French vines in less than twenty years. Other insect pests that attack and devour the leaves and the fruit of the vine do much harm and give the *vignerons* much trouble, but they can be checked. Not so the *Phylloxera vastatrix*, or vine louse; it hits the vine most unfairly, underground, below the belt, unseen, pinned to the roots of the vine and sucking its life-sap at source. There is but one sure method of fighting *phylloxera* with any chance of success: it is to flood the vineyard long enough to drown the bug, but not long enough to rot the roots of the vines. Unfortunately most vineyards responsible for wines of quality are hillside vineyards and cannot be flooded.

The *Phylloxera vastatrix* was first reported in Europe at Kew, near London, the famous Botanical Gardens, in a parcel of American native vines sent over as specimens. How this diabolical little pest managed to get from Kew, by the Thames, to Bordeaux, Burgundy and Champagne, to every vineyard of Europe and Africa, and to the island vineyards of the Mediterranean and of the Atlantic, nobody has ever been able to explain, but it did. By the end of the seventies os the last century, the vineyards of Bordeaux had been wiped out, and ten yeare later those of Burgundy and Champagne were dead or dying. Salvation came from the original home of phylloxera, the eastern states of North America, where native American species of vine had become, through centuries of co-habitation, nearly immune to phylloxera. Ever since, Cabernets, Pinots, Sauvignons, and all the other species of French vines have been grafted upon American phylloxera-resisting root-stocks. To replant millions of acres with these new 'franco-american' vines could only be done at a cost in hard cash and harder work which must have been staggering. But it was done, and the great vineyards of France still bring forth every year as great wines as ever before, whenever the sun is kind to them.

Are these wines really as great as before? Yes and no. Yes, if they are given the same chance as before to grow great gracefully. No, if they are drunk in far too great a hurry.

CHAPTER TWO

The Wines of Bordeaux

BORDEAUX IS, AFTER Marseilles, the oldest port of France – it welcomed Crassus and his Roman legions in 56 B.C.

Bordeaux, built upon the left bank of the River Garonne, some forty miles inland from the Atlantic, has never ceased to expand during the past two thousand years, mostly westwards, burying its own vineyards under a relentless tide of *chais*, shops and houses.

Bordeaux is the metropolis of the Gironde Département, the largest of the French Départements, some 104 miles long and 75 wide, with over 2,500 million acres of vineyards, forests, pastures, marshes and sandy dunes, and with a population of over a million ever-thirsty souls.

The Gironde Département takes its name from the River Gironde, a great tidal waterway, as much as 7 miles wide at its widest, and some 37 miles long, from the Bay of Biscay to the Bec d'Ambès, where La Garonne, from the south, and La Dordogne, from the north, meet and become La Gironde.

There are vineyards in most parts of the Gironde Département, vineyards which are expected to bring forth every year 203,000 *tonneaux* of red Bordeaux wine, and 153,500 *tonneaux* of white Bordeaux, 356,500 *tonneaux* in all, equal to 1,426,000 casks, or nearly 500,000,000 bottles of perfectly genuine Bordeaux wine – great, good or not so good wines, according to the soil of the vineyards and the whim of the weather.

Granting, as we must, that the best wine is the wine that we like best, there is no denying the fact that the vineyards of Bordeaux produce wines of the highest quality in greater quantities and also greater variety than any of the other vineyards of France. Quality is the result of the happy partnership between soil, vines and climate, conditions which may be, and are, just as favourable elsewhere; quantity is a matter of acres, and the Gironde Département is the largest of all Départements; variety is due to differences in the nature of the soil and sub soil of the vineyards as well as to differences in the species of the vines.

In the Gironde Département there is a very large number of different sorts of soil: silt and alluvial deposits have been brought down in the course of past centuries from the south by the Garonne, and from the east by the Dordogne; there are pockets, veins and streaks of clay, lime, sand, gravel, flint and all manner of different sorts of soils, either by themselves or mixed together in an almost infinite variety of proportion and location, upon higher or lower ground, facing the rising sun or the briny humidity from the Bay of Biscay.

Then there are the vines, and they are responsible, in the Gironde, for a greater measure of variety of both red and white wines than anywhere else. In Burgundy all the best red wines are made from Pinots noiriens and the best white wines from Pinots Chardonnay. In Alsace, different wines are made from different species of grapes, Sylvaner, Riesling, Traminer, etc. In the Gironde, however, the red wines are made from three or four different species of grapes, Cabernets chiefly, Malbec, Merlot and Verdot; and the white wines mostly from three different species of grapes, Semillon, Sauvignon and Muscadelle. Cabernet grapes for the red wines, and Semillon for the whites, are always used to a greater extent in the making of all the better wines, but the proportion may vary from as much as 95% to as little as 60% of the whole, and the choice of the other grapes used at the same time varies with almost every individual vineyard. This practice of making wine from different varieties of grapes is responsible for differences in "bouquet" and "body" of different wines; it is also responsible for their rate of maturing. A Mouton-Rothschild, for instance, made from 80% to 90% of Cabernet grapes will be "hard" and it will not have the same charm and appeal as another Pauillac wine made in the same year and in the same way from 65% Cabernets and 35% other grapes, that is, when both will be five or six years old; but, ten years later, the first will be a distinctly finer wine and after another twenty years it will probably be superb, a really great wine, whilst the other will be a poor, feeble, tottering old man.

Of all red table wines, the red wine of Bordeaux, which has been known in England by the name of *Claret* for quite a while – the past seven centuries – may be called the perfect wine; like the perfect wife, it looks nice and it is nice; natural, wholesome; ever helpful, yet not assertive; dependable always; gracious and gentle, but neither dumb, dull nor monotonous: a rare gift and a real joy.

The red wines of Bordeaux, more particularly the more *ordinaires* among them, are acceptable when quite young, when three or four years old, but not, like some Beaujolais red wines, for instance, when twelve or eighteen months old. On the other hand, there are no table wines in the world capable of standing the test of time as the wines of Bordeaux do. They certainly possess the "gift of age".

In October 1950, on Ian Campbell's 80th birthday, members of the Saintsbury Club dined at the Vintners' Hall in London and drank their last fifteen bottles of Lafite 1870, which the Cellarer had saved hopefully for that occasion. Three or four of the bottles were a little tired and one was vinegar, but that was the fault of the corks, not of the wine: all the other bottles were wonderful – a real joy. I have enjoyed older and even greater Lafites, 1858 and 1864 Lafite, but I never tasted the Lafite 1811 which Maurice Healy was given at Château Lafite in 1926, when he wrote that "at its age of 115 years it still drank graciously, with not more than a suspicion of fading".

No white wine will ever age as gracefully as the red, but the great white wines of Sauternes will outlive all other French white wines. At sixty years of age, in 1929, Yquem 1869 was still a truly magnificent wine.

The gift of age, which the wines of Bordeaux have enjoyed to such a remarkable extent, for so long, is due to the fact that they are made with sound grapes, ripe grapes, whole grapes, lots of them, and nothing else; they are made with greater care and leisure than art. The grapes are bruised, crushed and pressed as they are picked: their sweet juice ferments and becomes wine in its own sweet way; the new wine is left alone to grow slowly but surely into a grand wine. There is no sugar, no spirit, no sulphur, no lime, nothing added at any stage: the new wine is "racked" from time to time, i.e. moved from one cask away from its cast-off "lees" into a clean cask, and that is all the attention it needs until it is old enough to be bottled.

Today, the soil of the vineyards of the Gironde is the same as before: the grapes are also the same; it is true that since the phylloxera tragedy the old French vines have to be grafted upon American bug-resisting root-stock, but they have proved abundantly that Claret is as good as it ever was. Château Latour 1899 and Château Margaux 1900, for instance, were still very great wines when I last tasted them, in 1954, and so was the 1899 Château Pontet-Canet which I was privileged to drink, in March 1956, at Pontet-Canet. What has changed so much is the demand. The faster our means of transport, the more time do we save, and yet the faster the tempo of life, the less leisure do we have. There are fewer and fewer wine-lovers who are prepared or able to lay down wine of a good vintage and forget about it for twenty years, as used to be a common practice not so very long ago. Everything is against it: the considerably higher "starting price" of wine – that is, its original cost at the time of the vintage, is the first limiting factor: then there is the lack of proper storage space now that great houses are all but impossible to staff and to live in. Most people today have no choice, even had they the wish, but to buy wine for drinking on the same day, or within a matter of weeks or of months, not of years. Inevitably the supply must adapt itself to the demand, and the wines of today must be made, and can be made, to be ready for drinking with a minimum of maturing. This can be done without any magic or chemicals, simply by using a different technique. To begin with, when the bunches of ripe grapes are picked, they are now égrappées, that is, put through a kind of callender-drum which tears away the berries from the husks – the frame upon which they were attached from birth. These husks are separated and thrown out, so that the vegetable acids which they contain, like all vegetable living substances, do not get into the wine. The wine can do without them perfectly well, but they introduce an element of acidity, undesirable at first, and yet helpful to make the wine keep its freshness in old age. Then, when the grapes are pressed, the fermentation of their sweet juice can be slowed down or accelerated by longer or shorter periods in the open *"Cuves"*, or great vats, where all wines are born and have their fill of fresh air before being locked up in barrels, with much less breathing space and air. It is thus possible for Bordeaux wines to be "ready" or fit to drink when still quite young, from four to six years old, although they should be much better, of course, if given another five or even ten years to "grow up".

Château Bottling

It is the immediate concern and paramount responsibility of all Châteaux owners to grow good grapes and to make good wine: how the wine was to be "nursed", and when it should be bottled, used to be left to the merchants: it was their business, and a most important one indeed. There was a time, a hundred years or so ago, when a vintage Claret was sold as vintage Port was sold until much more recently, with the name of the wine-merchant responsible for the bottling. One can still see upon some of the catalogues of wine auctions two lots of Claret offered for sale, both of the same Château and of the same vintage, one Château-bottled and the other bottled in England or in Scotland by some English or Scottish wine-merchant well-known at the time. I remember one such sale when the English-bottling fetched a higher price than the Château-bottling of the same wine, evidently because it was a better wine. In those days, the status of the family wine-merchant was that of the family doctor and the family solicitor: he was implicitly trusted, and to deserve the trust placed in him he had to give his clients wines which were to their liking; he also gave them very long credit. It was quite normal for a perfectly honest wine-merchant to "improve" the Claret which he had received from Bordeaux, and I have seen an invoice of the early thirties – of the last century – from one of the most highly respected Leith wine-merchants, for some Lafite Hermitaged. There was no vintage mentioned and the wine may have been that of a poor year, or a blend of two indifferent vintages, which had been "improved" by the addition of a good, stout, red Hermitage. There was no deception.

Château bottling was at first occasionally demanded by and accorded to a few rather fussy merchants who were anxious to offer a wine that could not be suspected of having been blended, or "cut", as it was called at the time. It was in 1869, when the vintage was small but very good, that the whole of the wine made at Château Lafite was "Château bottled" for the first time. Of course, the mere physical act of bottling a wine in the Château's *Chais* or Cellars is by no means sufficient to entitle the wine to call itself "Château bottled": this is a privilege which the owner of the Château may grant or not, at his will. When he grants it, the corks used at the bottling time are branded with the name of the Château and the year of the vintage; later on, when the bottles are "dressed", the labels will bear the mention "Mise en bouteille du Château" or "Mis en bouteilles au Château".

Until quite recent times, the "Château bottling" was not granted by all the Châteaux: there were some who never gave the "Château bottling", whilst others granted it now and again, when they considered that the vintage was an exceptionally fine one. Lately, however, "Château bottling" has become the rule instead of the exception. Some Châteaux, like Mouton-Rothschild, do their own bottling: they sell none of their wine in cask but bottled at the Château in half-bottles, bottles, magnums, and larger bottles which are numbered from "one" upwards so that each can always be identified in whatever part of the world it may eventually stray before its cork be released and its contents deliver their glad message.

"Château bottling" still is what it has always been: a birth certificate, but it can no longer be regarded as necessarily a certificate of merit.

The Gironde

There are vineyards in all parts of the Bordeaux country and it is difficult to decide which might be the best way to visit them. Let us begin with the Gironde, the greatest of the three waterways of the Département that bears its name; we shall next turn to the Garonne and lastly to the Dordogne.

There are many vineyards along both banks of the Gironde, as well as in the islands, large and small, amidstream: they are responsible for about 33% of the total wine production of the Département, that is wine entitled to the proud name of Bordeaux, 40% of all the red wines and 25% of all the whites. The vineyards upon the left bank of the Gironde which produce most of the best red wines as well as a greater quantity than the vineyards of the Garonne and Dordogne are the vineyards of the Médoc, and they account for 22% of the total vinous production of the Département, but only 1% of its white wines. The vineyards upon the right bank of the Gironde, those of Bourg and Blaye, as well as the vineyards of the Gironde islands, produce 18% of all the red wines and 24% of all the white wines, none of them, however, comparable in quality to the best wines of the Médoc.

The Médoc

Médoc was originally the name given to all the country that stretches from the Garonne, above Bordeaux, and from the Gironde, westwards and northwards, as far as the Bay of Biscay. All along the Médoc seaboard, and for some miles inland, there are sand dunes, fir trees, heath and grass lands, lakes and marshes, but no vines. The vineyards of the Médoc have always been along its eastern fringe, some of them in Palus close to the Garonne or Gironde, and the others, all the better ones, upon higher ground called Graves on account of the gravelly nature of the soil.

Both Palus and Graves vineyards of the Médoc are of alluvial origin, but not of the same age. The Palus are of comparatively recent formation, and they are rich in silt deposits: their vines bear more grapes than those planted in Graves vineyards, but their wines are not nearly so good: they never have the *finesse* or breed and charm of Graves-grown wines. The Graves vineyards of the Médoc are also of alluvial origin, but of much more remote antiquity; in the main they follow the courses of Garonne and Gironde, only the last few miles of the first but nearly the whole of the Gironde, upon a succession of ridges which vary both in height and width: more important still is the fact that the depth of this precious grit-cum-sand-cum-pebbles Graves soil also varies very much, from a few inches in some parts to as much as ten feet in others.

It was only in the course of the eighteenth century that the use of the name Médoc became restricted to the land lying north of the Jalle de Blanquefort (a jalle is a small stream), and westwards, to the Atlantic. It was also then that the name Graves ceased to be used for those wines of the Médoc made from grapes grown on Graves soil, and was reserved for those of the vineyards south of Blanquefort, on the left bank of the Garonne.

The Médoc, which now begins a little more than five miles north of Bordeaux, is divided into upper and lower, Haut-Médoc and Bas-Médoc. The first comprised twenty-nine Communes, the vineyards of which were and still are responsible for all the finer wines, and the second twenty-three Communes producing mostly *vins ordinaires*. During the Second World War, the people of the geographically lower reaches of the Gironde objected to the name of Bas-Médoc and demanded that *Bas* be deleted, which was granted to them. So now plain Médoc officially means the northern or lower part of the old Médoc, whilst the southern part has retained its name of Haut-Médoc. All the greatest Médoc wines come from the Châteaux of the Haut-Médoc, most of them in the Communes of Margaux, Cantenac, Saint-Julien, Pauillac, and Saint Estèphe. There are, in the Haut-Médoc, about five hundred "Châteaux" or Estates, the vineyards of which are capable of producing 10,500 *tonneaux* of red wines or Claret every year, wines of fair, fine and very good quality, besides about 15,500 *tonneaux* of commoner red wines, and only about 415 *tonneaux* of white wine.

Many attempts have been made to grade the wines of the Châteaux du Médoc, and the "Classification" which still stands today after a hundred years was made in 1855, when four Châteaux were given first place, (although the fourth, Château Haut-Brion was included in spite of being in the Commune of Pessac in the Graves de Bordeaux district, not in Médoc); fifteen second, fourteen third, ten fourth and seventeen fifth. This Classification was drawn up at the request of the Bordeaux Chamber of Commerce by a number of Bordeaux brokers whose experience and integrity were universally acknowledged at the time. The Classification, now a hundred years old, was based on the prices paid by the merchants of Bordeaux for the wines of different vineyards during the best part of a century before 1855; it was considered safe enough to assume that the better the wine the higher would be the price that the merchants would pay for it. Up to 1820 the practice of the Bordeaux trade had been to recognise four main grades of Médoc *crus*, paying for the second growths approximately a fourth less than the price paid for the first; for the third, one fifth less than the price paid for the second; and for the fourth, one fifth less than the price paid for the third. In 1824, when Wm. Franck published his *Traité sur les vins du Médoc*, he placed in a fifth class the *crus* which had been hitherto known in Bordeaux as "*Deuxièmes quatrièmes Crus*" and this division was adopted, in 1855, by the brokers for the official classification. Although the quality of all wines must necessarily depend in the first place upon the geological formation of the soil and subsoil of each vineyard, which is why the 1855 Classification has stood the test of time so well, it must also be recognised that the care and skill of generations of *vignerons* may quite possibly make some difference for better or worse.

Today, for instance, most if not all Claret lovers would unhesitatingly vote for moving up Château Mouton-Rothschild from the top of the second *crus* to the first. I, for one, and I am sure that I would not be alone, would like to move up Palmer and Calon-Ségur from third to second, Talbot and Beychevelle from fourth to third or second, Pontet-Canet and Cantemerle from fifth to third or perhaps, second. But I would not hesitate to demote at least half a dozen other "classed" growths and replace them by excellent *Bourgeois Supérieurs* more deserving to be "*classés*" among the fifth growths, Châteaux Meyney, Sénéjac, Lanessan and Le Boscq to begin with.

Next to the "*Crus Classés*", in point of the excellence of their wines, come four Estates of the Haut-Médoc, which are known as *Crus Exceptionnels*, and immediately after them there are some two hundred *Crus Bourgeois Supérieurs*, most of them capable of producing very good wines indeed, often better value than some of the "Classed" growths, which are dearer but not invariably better.

The *Crus Classés*, the *Crus Exceptionnels* and the *Crus Bourgeois Supérieurs* of the Haut-Médoc are responsible for all the finer red wines of the Médoc, but there are a great many more vineyards which produce a much greater quantity of wines, mostly wines which cannot compete with the rest in the matter of breed and charm, yet quite pleasant and most acceptable table wines of the *"ordinaire"* and even *"grand ordinaire"* classes. There is also a number of gradings among them, the better ones being known as *Crus Bourgeois* and the others as *Crus Artisans*. There are also the *Vins de Palus*, from vineyards by the river-side or in the Gironde islands, and the *Vins de Terrefort*, from vineyards where clay takes the place of gravel.

Provided the weather happens to be all that it should be, that is when the sun shines and the rain comes at the right time and in due measure, the vineyards of the Haut-Médoc may be expected to produce the following quantities of wine in a year:—

	Tonneaux
Crus Classés	4,503
Crus Exceptionnels & Crus Bourgeois Supérieurs	6,019
Crus Bourgeois et Crus Artisans	12,821
Vins de Palus et de Terrefort	2,835
Vins blancs	415
	26,593 tonneaux

Communes, or Parishes, of the Haut-Médoc and their Châteaux

(the complete 1855 classification of the wines of the Médoc will be found in Appendix 2)

Starting from Bordeaux, to visit the vineyards of the Haut-Médoc, we shall leave the city by the Barrière du Médoc, pass by the Bordeaux football ground and the race course and bear right, after 7 km., leaving the more direct road to the Pointe de Grave, the main road, for what is known as *La Route des Châteaux du Médoc*. After 9 km. we shall cross a small stream, La Jalle de Blanquefort, which divides at this point the Graves country from the Haut-Médoc. Proceeding in a n.n.w. general direction, with at first the last few miles of the Garonne, and then the whole length of the Gironde on our right, we shall pass through all the Communes of the Haut-Médoc before reaching and passing through those of the Bas-Médoc, now called Médoc, *tout court*.

BLANQUEFORT (10 km. n.n.w. Bordeaux)

About one-third of the Blanquefort red wines are Palus wines from riverside vineyards. Château Tujean, the only Estate of importance, is one of the *Crus Bourgeois*.

LE TAILLAN (11 km. n.w. Bordeaux)

Château du Taillan is a modest *Cru Bourgeois*, but the Château itself is one of the finest of the Médoc; it is owned by, and is the residence of, Monsieur and Madame Jean Cruse. Its vineyards, the most important of the Commune, produced none but red wines until the early part of the present century, when white Semillon, Sauvignon and Muscadelle grapes were planted: ever since this Château's vines have produced on an average 50 *tonneaux* of red wine, sold as Château du Taillan, and 20 *tonneaux* of white wine, sold as Château Dame-Blanche.

SAINT-MÉDARD-EN-JALLES (13 km. n.w. Bordeaux)

One of the less important Communes of the Haut-Médoc: its *Crus Bourgeois* vineyards produce an average of 50 *tonneaux* of fair red wines, and its other vineyards about 150 *tonneaux* of quite *ordinaires* red wines.

SAINT-AUBIN (15 km. n.w. Bordeaux)

About forty small *vignerons* make on an average from 1 to 6 *tonneaux* of red wine each, every year. The only vineyard of any size is that of Château de Cujac.

PAREMPUYRE (16 km. n. Bordeaux)

There are in this Commune two *Bourgeois Supérieurs*: one is the Château Ségur, operated by M. J. Grazioli for the Société Agricole du Château Ségur; the other is Cru Ségur-Fillon owned by M. J. Grazioli. These *Crus Bourgeois Supérieurs* are responsible for some 40 *tonneaux* of good red wines, whilst the riverside Palus vineyards produce about twice as much *ordinaires* red wines. The only white vineyard is M. Georges Guestier's *Clos Mon-Blanc*.

LUDON (16 km. n. Bordeaux)

In Ludon there is a *Troisième Cru Classé*, Château Grand-La-Lagune, better known outside France as Château La Lagune, which produces an average of 200 *tonneaux* of excellent red wine. The prosperity of the Commune, however, rests mostly upon its riverside Palus vineyards which are responsible for an average of 600 *tonneaux* of more *ordinaires* but popular red wines. There are also eight *Crus Bourgeois Supérieurs* with an average aggregate production of 110 *tonneaux*. Also 200 *tonneaux* of less distinguished red wines from *Crus Bourgeois* and *Crus Artisans*.

LE PIAN-MÉDOC (17 km. n. Bordeaux)

This Commune, immediately west of both Parempuyre and Ludon, further away from the river, has only one notable Estate, the Château Sénéjac, a *Cru*

Bourgeois Supérieur, which produces some 60 *tonneaux* of a very elegant red wine. Other vineyards are responsible for a further 100 *tonneaux* of red and 10 *tonneaux* of white wines.

MACAU (21 km. n. Bordeaux)

Macau is a very important Commune of the Haut-Médoc both quantitatively and qualitatively. Its pride is the Château Cantemerle, the home of that grand old man of the Gironde, M. Jean Dubos. Cantemerle was placed last of the fifth growths, in 1855, but the 100 *tonneaux* of red wine which it produces on an average usually fetch and deserve higher prices than most wines of the fourth and third growths. The "second wine" of Cantemerle is sold under the registered name of *Royal Médoc*. There are no less than nine *Crus Bourgeois Supérieurs* in Macau, which are responsible for an average yield of 240 *tonneaux* of very fair red wine, besides Palus vineyards producing an average of 1,000 *tonneaux* of sound red wines and some *Crus Bourgeois*, *Artisans* and Terrefort producing 200 *tonneaux* of red wines. The three small white vineyards of Château Larrieu-Blanc, Priban and Maucamps, produce·5 *tonneaux* of white wines each.

ARSAC [1] (22 km. n.w. Bordeaux)

Arsac, immediately west of Macau, is a smaller Commune with one *Cinquième Cru Classé*, Château Du Tertre, with a yield of 100 *tonneaux* of good red wine; two *Crus Bourgeois Supérieurs*, Château d'Arsac, which produces 20 *tonneaux* of red and 10 *tonneaux* of white wines; and Château Monbrison with a yield of 40 *tonneaux* of red wine.

LABARDE [1] (24 km. n.n.w. Bordeaux)

Labarde lies east of Arsac, west and north of Macau and south of Cantenac. There are two *Crus Classés* in Labarde, a third Château Giscours, (200 *tonneaux*), and a fifth Château Dauzac, (100 *tonneaux*), their vineyards overflow into the adjoining Commune of Cantenac and their wines may be sold as Margaux wines. There are also in Labarde three *Crus Bourgeois Supérieurs*, of which the more important is Château Siran (100 *tonneaux*).

Château Dauzac was the property of one of the more important firms of Bordeaux merchants during the greater part of the nineteenth and the early part of the twentieth century, Messrs. Nathaniel Johnston & Cie: they not only made good wine but they made it one of the best known Clarets in the U.S.A. and the United Kingdom.

CANTENAC [1] (25 km. n. Bordeaux)

The vineyards of Cantenac and those of nearby Margaux produce some of the

[1] The *Crus classés* of Arsac, Labarde and Cantenac have been given the *Appellation Contrôlée* 'Margaux'.

most delightful red wines of the Médoc and of the world. There are no less than seven *Crus Classés* in the Commune of Cantenac: one second, Château Brane-Cantenac (200 *tonneaux*); four thirds, Châteaux, Kirwan (60 *tonneaux*), d'Issan (80 *tonneaux*), Cantenac-Brown (70 *tonneaux*), and Palmer (120 *tonneaux*); and two fourths, Châteaux Le Prieuré-Lichine (75 *tonneaux*) and Pouget (20 *tonneaux*).

Château d'Issan is one of the finest examples of mediaeval architecture of the Gironde. The great building, which is surrounded by a very wide moat, and its vineyards were, most unfortunately, sadly neglected for some years until the end of the last war when the property was acquired by M. Emmanuel Cruse. The old castle has now been put into good repair and some of its best vineyards have been replanted. Formerly, there were many acres of vines on lower land, on the Gironde side of the Château, which produced large quantities of inexpensive *Bourgeois* Claret, sold as *Moulin d'Issan*: those acres are now under grass and the farm of the Château d'Issan is one of the more important of the Médoc.

Château Palmer was known for a very long time as a popular wine under the name of *Château de Gasq*. It was acquired in or about 1820 by one of Louis XVIII's generals, named Palmer, who gave it his name. Château Palmer bears on its label the name of Margaux, not Cantenac, and other Châteaux of the Cantenac Commune do the same, when some of their vineyards, like those of Château Palmer, are partly in the Margaux Commune.

The vineyard of Château Le Prieuré, formerly known as Cantenac-Prieuré, was planted at the beginning of the seventeenth century by the Prior of Cantenac. The Château and its vines were acquired in 1952 by Alexis Lichine, since when Cantenac-Prieuré has been renamed Prieuré-Lichine.

Of the four *Crus Bourgeois Supérieurs* of Cantenac, the most important is Château Angludet (60 *tonneaux*) and the most unfortunate is Château Montbrun (40 *tonneaux*), owned by M. René Lebègue, which was destroyed by fire in 1954. There are also about 20 *tonneaux* of white wines made from Cantenac vineyards, 10 *tonneaux* are sold under the registered name *Château Montbrun Goutte d'Or* and 10 *tonneaux* as *Château Cantenac-Blanc*.

MARGAUX (28 km. n.w. Bordeaux)

Margaux is one of the most universally known of all the Communes of the Haut-Médoc, and its many vineyards produce a considerable quantity of red wine, as well as a very little white wine. All the best red wines of Margaux possess a distinctive and very attractive *bouquet* that is quite impossible to describe in mere words; it is somewhat reminiscent of what might be wild violets-cum-amber perfume.

Plate 3 BORDEAUX. Ripe old age. As the wine grows older, it fades from ruby to a dark brick red, as may be seen from this picture of Château Lafite 1887, decanted into an old French decanter. The seal or glass "button" on the shoulder of the bottle was used by Bordeaux shippers when Châteaux owners refused to grant the right to use corks branded with the name of the Château and the year of the vintage, the official seal of the Château bottling privilege.

The pride of the Commune of Margaux is, of course, Château Margaux, *le roi du Médoc*, as it has been called, and one of the four *Premiers Crus*. It is certainly one of the show places of the Médoc; the Château itself is a very handsome mansion built in 1802 by the Marquis de la Colonille who pulled down what was left of the former Château de Lamothe, a *château fort* of the fifteenth century. It was bought in 1870 by the Comte Pillet-Will, whose heirs sold it in 1920, and during the fifty years of what may be called the Pillet-Will régime, the wine of Château Margaux was always as fine as that of the other three first growths and occasionally the best of them all. There was never a finer 1871, for instance, than the Château Margaux of that vintage. It was light, both in colour and texture, at sixty years old, when I last tasted it, but still possessing a delicate yet penetrating and typically "Margaux" *bouquet;* it was sweet to the end; ethereal, fascinating, perfect. In 1888, not a great year in the Médoc, Château Margaux stood out lengths ahead of the "field": it was not really great but it was delicious. Then there was the 1900 Château Margaux, which won first place by a very short head – all 1900's were so good! There have also been times, unfortunately, more particularly between the last two wars, when Château Margaux failed to live up to its very high standard of excellence, but its present owner, M. Pierre Ginestet, is determined never to allow that to happen again.

Château Margaux, as one approaches it along an avenue of fine trees, has great dignity and beauty, but the great *chai* of the Château, close to it, has even greater majesty as one enters it. The vineyards of Château Margaux produce on an average 180 *tonneaux* of first-class red wine, besides a smaller quantity of red wines sold as *Pavillon rouge de Château Margaux*.

There are four *Deuxièmes*, four *Troisièmes* and one *Quatrième Crus Classés* in the Commune of Margaux. The *Deuxièmes Crus* are: Château Rausan-Ségla (70 *tonneaux*) Château Rauzan-Gassies (60 *tonneaux*); Château Durfort (80 *tonneaux*); and Château Lascombes (200 *tonneaux*), now owned by a syndicate of American financiers.

The *Troisièmes Crus Classés* are: Châteaux Malescot-Saint-Exupéry (80 *tonneaux*) and Marquis d'Alesme-Becker (40 *tonneaux*); Château Ferrière (20 *tonneaux*); and Château Desmirail (30 *tonneaux*).

The *Quatrième Cru Classé* is Château Marquis de Terme (150 *tonneaux*).

There are five *Crus Bourgeois Supérieurs* in the Commune of Margaux; their average annual production is 150 *tonneaux* of very decent red wine. *Crus Bourgeois* and *Artisans* are responsible for a further quantity of 150 *tonneaux* of more *ordinaires* red wines, and the riverside Palus vineyards for some 200 *tonneaux* of commoner wines. There are also some 25 *tonneaux* of white wines made from the white grapes of Château Margaux; they are sold under the name of *Pavillon blanc de Château Margaux*.

Plate 4 BORDEAUX. The Médoc: Château Pontet-Canet, Pauillac.
Typical of the Médoc châteaux amid vineyards planted in pebbly, sandy
soil rising from the left bank of the Gironde.

From Margaux to Moulis, westwards, there are four Communes of little vinous importance:

AVENSAN (29 km. n.w. Bordeaux)

Its best vineyard is that of Château Villegeorge (50 *tonneaux*), whilst five small *Crus Bourgeois Supérieurs* produce an average of 135 *tonneaux* of fair red wines; and *Bourgeois* and *Artisans* a further 300 tonneaux of commoner wines.

CASTELNAU (28 km. n.w. Bordeaux)

Its vineyards are responsible for an average of 100 *tonneaux* of *ordinaires, Bourgeois* or *Artisans* wines.

SOUSSANS (30 km. n.n.w. Bordeaux)

Its best vineyard is that of Château Bel-Air-Marquis d'Aligre (50 *tonneaux*), a *Cru exceptionnel*. There are four *Crus Bourgeois Supérieurs* with an aggregate yield of 165 *tonneaux* of very fair red wines, much the largest of them being the Château La Tour de Mons (100 *tonneaux*), the property of Monsieur Dubos.

ARCINS (33 km. n. Bordeaux)

There are no vineyards of particular excellence in this Commune, which produces about 250 *tonneaux* of *ordinaires* red wines from *Crus Bourgeois* and *Artisans*.

MOULIS (33 km. n. Bordeaux)

This is an important Commune with no less than twenty-one *Crus Bourgeois Supérieurs*, producing an aggregate of over 700 *tonneaux* of sound, dependable, pleasant red wines. The best vineyard of Moulis is that of Château Chasse-Spleen (180 *tonneaux*), a *Cru Exceptionnel*.

LISTRAC (34 km. n.w. Bordeaux)

This Commune is chiefly noted for the large quantity (1,000 *tonneaux*) of *ordinaires* but pleasing and dependable red wines, *Crus Bourgeois* and *Artisans*, sold as *Listrac* and also under the name of *Château Grand Listrac*. There is no such Château, but it is the registered name under which the wines of the *Co-opérative des Producteurs de Listrac* are sold.

There are, however, some better Listrac wines: they are those from the dozen *Crus Bourgeois Supérieurs* of the Commune – 625 *tonneaux* in all.

LAMARQUE (36 km. n.w. Bordeaux)

Lamarque is one of the less important Communes of the Haut-Médoc. Its three *Crus Bourgeois Supérieurs* produce an average of 220 *tonneaux* of fair quality red wines, and its *Crus Bourgeois* and *Artisans* a further 350 *tonneaux* of *ordinaires* wines.

CUSSAC (33 km. n.n.w. Bordeaux)

This is also one of the minor Haut-Médoc Communes, with four *Crus Bourgeois Supérieurs*, producing an aggregate of 230 *tonneaux* of fair red wines, the wine of Château Lanessan (100 *tonneaux*) being probably the best and certainly the best-known of the four. The *Crus Bourgeois* and *Crus Artisans* produce an average of 500 *tonneaux* of *ordinaires* wines.

SAINT-LAURENT (43 km. n.n.w. Bordeaux)

This Commune has three of the *Crus Classés:* Château La Tour-Carnet (80 *tonneaux*), a *Quatrième Cru*; Château Belgrave (120 *tonneaux*), a *Cinquième Cru*; and Château Camensac (100 *tonneaux*), also a *Cinquième Cru*.

The *Crus Bourgeois Supérieurs* of Saint-Laurent are four in number and produce an aggregate of 610 *tonneaux* of very fair red wines: the best known is Château Ballac (200 *tonneaux*). The *Crus Bourgeois* and *Artisans* produce 500 *tonneaux* of *ordinaires* red wines and 100 *tonneaux* of undistinguished white wines.

SAINT-JULIEN (44 km. n.n.w. Bordeaux)

Back again, nearer the Gironde, we come to one of the most universally known Communes of the Haut-Médoc, Saint-Julien-Beychevelle, better known as Saint-Julien. Its vineyards produce a very large quantity of red wines of superlative excellence, which possess a unique delicate "tenderness" or silkiness of body as well as a most attractive *bouquet*.

There are twelve *Crus Classés* in the Commune of Saint-Julien, including five of the most popular *Deuxièmes Crus*, the Châteaux Léoville-Las-Cases (200 *tonneaux*); Léoville-Poyferré (170 *tonneaux*); Léoville-Barton (100 *tonneaux*); Gruaud-Larose (200 *tonneaux*); and Ducru-Beaucaillou (200 *tonneaux*).

Château Gruaud-Larose is not one of the oldest Châteaux of the Médoc: it dates back merely to 1757. The daughter of the original Monsieur Gruaud married a Monsieur de Larose and the Château became Gruaud-Larose until 1812 when it was sold to Baron Sarget, and was eventually divided among his heirs, which is why there were two Châteaux Gruaud-Larose during the best part of a century, one called Gruaud-Larose-Sarget and the other Gruaud-Larose-Faure. Recently, however, both parts of the original property were acquired by M. Desiré Cordier, since when there has been once more the one and only Château Gruaud-Larose.

The two *Troisièmes Crus* of Saint-Julien are Châteaux Lagrange (200 *tonneaux*) and Château Langoa-Barton (100 *tonneaux*). The five *Quatrièmes Crus* of Saint-

Julien are Châteaux Saint-Pierre Bontemps (75 *tonneaux*) joined with Saint-Pierre Sevaistre, Branaire-Ducru (150 *tonneaux*), Talbot (300 *tonneaux*) and Beychevelle (150 *tonneaux*).

Château Talbot is one of the finest Estates of the Médoc with, besides a splendid vineyard, a model farm and a famous stud. The Château itself is a modern and very handsome mansion which, according to tradition, stands on the site of the mediaeval castle which, five hundred years ago, was the home and headquarters of the brave and ill-fated Talbot who was killed at Castillon, near Libourne, in 1453.

The wine of Château Talbot has ranked among the best of the Médoc for many centuries, but its fame was never greater than during the eighteenth century when the Château was owned by the Marquis d'Aux – which is why it is also called Talbot d'Aux.[1] It is now owned by M. Georges Cordier.

Château Beychevelle, the residence of M. Achille Fould, is a very charming house in a delightful setting. It stands on the site of the Château of the hereditary Grand Admirals of France whom ships had to salute by lowering their sails as they passed by on their way to or from Bordeaux. Beychevelle also had, until recent times, a port of its own on the Gironde, but it became silted up and its place was taken by the port of Pauillac, a little farther downstream. The Commune of Beychevelle lost much of its former importance when it lost its port, and it was eventually merged with its neighbour Saint-Julien, the full administrative name of which is Saint-Julien-Beychevelle.

There are surprisingly enough only two *Bourgeois Supérieurs* with an average aggregate production of 208 *tonneaux* of very fair red wine – Châteaux du Glana (200 *tonneaux*) and Bontemps-Dubarry (8 *tonneaux*). The *Crus Bourgeois* and *Artisans* of the Commune produce some 250 *tonneaux* of the more *ordinaires* St Julien red wines. The only St Julien white wine is that of Château Sirène-Lagrange (10 *tonneaux*).

PAUILLAC (48 km. n.n.w. Bordeaux)

Pauillac is a more important village, almost a town, with nearly 6,000 inhabitants and a port which is second only to Bordeaux. Although its name has nothing like the world-wide popularity of St Julien and St Estèphe, the two Communes immediately to the south and to the north of Pauillac, it is the only Commune of the Haut-Médoc with two *Premiers Crus*, Lafite and Latour, besides the first of the *Deuxièmes Crus*, Château Mouton-Rothschild, which is today the peer of the *Premiers Crus*.

---

[1]   The poet Biarnez reversed the order:
'Tout ce qu'un quatrième a de charme et de grâce
Résume d'Aux Talbot la gloire de sa classe.'

Château Lafite, or Lafite-Rothschild to give it its full name, is one of the oldest of the Châteaux du Médoc and its wines have on numerous occasions been placed ahead of all others. Lafite 1864, for instance, was quite outstanding for fully half a century, and it outlived all the other great wines of that great vintage. As late as the early thirties, when it was very nearly seventy years old, Lafite 1864 was wonderful: it was still fresh, soft and sweet, and its exquisite *bouquet* made one pause and wonder whether there is any age limit to a really great Claret. The Lafite 1869 was not so well known as the '64; there was very much less of it, but it was an astounding wine. We had a bottle of it given to us by Dr O. W. Loeb for our Golden Wedding, in October 1950, straight from the Château. We gave it a long rest and drank it in 1954: it was incredibly good! Not merely alive but lively; ruby red, not pink; fairly sweet still; very smooth, gentle and charming, its *bouquet* discreet but intensely clean, without any trace of "dead leaves" not objectionable in very old wines, but a warning that the end is at hand!

The Lafite 1870 also lasted almost "for ever", but it was always somewhat hard. It had more power than grace, so unlike all other Lafites of that generation that one could not help identifying it at once. But I failed to do so, once. It was in 1932, at Wistler's Wood, when we were the guests of Gus Mayer. He gave us a bottle of Lafite 1870, not Château bottled, but bottled at Bordeaux by Nathaniel Johnston. It was perfect, so free from tannin, and so gracious, that I believed then and still believe now that it had been "cut" or blended with the Lafite 1871, which was a honeyed wine.

After phylloxera and the replanting of the Lafite vineyards, there was no Château bottling granted from 1885 to 1905, in spite of the fact that Lafite 1895 was by far the best wine of the year. Lafite 1899 and 1900 were also two very good wines, although Latour, Margaux and Mouton were even better. In more recent years, Château Lafite 1924's and 1953's have been quite outstanding and voted the best of their vintage. The average yield of Lafite is 200 *tonneaux*, a truly amazing quantity of wine of outstanding merit.

Château Latour, with an average production of 250 *tonneaux*, is the other *Premier Cru Classé* of Pauillac. Its wines are extremely reliable, either the best or second best of the year, and never disappointing. The Latour 1878, 1899 and 1920 were distinctly finer wines than all others, but in my own experience, whenever any other *Premier* or *Deuxième Cru* is given first place, Latour is always very near the top.

Mouton was placed at the top of the *Deuxièmes Crus* in the 1855 Classification, but such care has been taken of its vineyards and of its wines that it would certainly be placed among the *Premiers Crus* today. The fact that ever since 1929 the wines of Château Mouton-Rothschild have always fetched in the open market the same price as, or a higher price than the wines of the *Premiers Crus* of the same vintage, is sufficient evidence of its excellence. Its average annual yield is 250 tonneaux.

There are, in Pauillac, two other *Deuxièmes Crus*, Châteaux Pichon-Longueville (100 *tonneaux*) and Pichon-Longueville-Comtesse de Lalande[1] (160 *tonneaux*) Also one *Quatrième Cru*, Château Duhart-Milon (140 *tonneaux*), and ten *Cinquièmes Crus*: Châteaux Pontet-Canet (400 *tonneaux*), the property and the summer residence of the Cruse family; Batailley (200 *tonneaux*); Haut-Batailley (70 *tonneaux*); Grand-Puy-Ducasse (40 *tonneaux*); Grand-Puy-Lacoste (100 *tonneaux*). Lynch-Bages (200 *tonneaux*); Mouton Baron Philippe (so renamed in 1963) (150 *tonneaux*); Croizet-Bages (60 *tonneaux*); Pédesclaux (60 *tonneaux*); and Clerc-Milon-Mondon (50 *tonneaux*). Châteaux Lynch-Moussas and Haut-Bages-Libéral have ceased production.

There are in the commune of Pauillac, nineteen *Crus Bourgeois Supérieurs* with an aggregate production of 700 *tonneaux* of fine red wines. The *Crus Bourgeois* and *Artisans* are responsible for 1,000 *tonneaux* of more *ordinaires* wines, which are mostly sold under the name of *Grand Vin La Rose Pauillac, Haut-Médoc*, a name registered by the *Co-opérative de Propriétaires Viticulteurs de Pauillac*.

SAINT-SAUVEUR (6 km. w. Pauillac)

There are in this Commune three *Crus Bourgeois Supérieurs*: Châteaux Fontestau (60 *tonneaux*), Liversan (70 *tonneaux*), and Peyrabon (200 *tonneaux*); and an average of 300 *tonneaux* of more *ordinaires* red wines from *Crus Bourgeois* and *Artisans* which are mostly made, handled and sold by the *Co-opérative de Saint-Sauveur Haut-Médoc*.

CISSAC (55 km. n.n.w. Bordeaux)

The *Cave Co-opérative de Cissac-Haut-Médoc* handles the grapes of some 80 small *vignerons* of the Commune at the Château Cissac, the residence of M. and Mme. Louis Vialard.

SAINT-ESTÈPHE (57 km. n.n.w. Bordeaux)

The Commune of Saint-Estèphe is one of the four most important wine-producing Communes of the Haut-Médoc. Its wines have a distinctive character of their own, rather more weight and substance than those of Saint-Julien or Margaux, and a *bouquet* rather more earthy.

There are, in the Commune of Saint-Estèphe, two *Deuxièmes Crus*, Châteaux Cos d'Estournel (200 *tonneaux*), and Montrose (240 *tonneaux*); one *Troisième Cru*, Château Calon-Ségur (200 *tonneaux*); one *Quatrième Cru*, Château Rochet (100 *tonneaux*), and one *Cinquième Cru*, Château Cos-Labory (40 *tonneaux*).

---

[1] This Château has been given the *Appellation Contrôlée* 'Saint-Julien'.

There are also no less than 30 *Crus Bourgeois Supérieurs*, the aggregate production of which averages 1,850 *tonneaux* of stout, sound, reliable red wines.

The *Cave Co-opérative de Saint-Estèphe* handles the grapes and wines of about 140 small *vignerons*, an average of some 560 *tonneaux* in all.

VERTHEUIL (56 km. n.n.w. Bordeaux)

The *Crus Bourgeois* and *Artisans* of this Commune produce 500 *tonneaux* of red wine. The only white wine of Vertheuil, Château Reysson, averages 10 *tonneaux*. *The Cave Co-opérative de Vertheuil* handles the grapes and wines of about 60 small *vignerons*.

SAINT-SEURIN-DE-CADOURNE (13 km. Pauillac)

The northernmost Commune of the Haut-Médoc, 13 km. from both Lesparre and Pauillac. Its *Crus Bourgeois* and *Artisans* produce 1,000 *tonneaux* of wine. The *Cave Co-opérative de Saint-Seurin-de-Cadourne* handles the grapes and wines of about 60 small *vignerons;* their wines are sold under the registered name of *La-Paroisse-Saint-Seurin-Haut-Médoc*.

Bas-Médoc (now called Médoc)

Beyond Saint-Seurin-de-Cadourne, as one proceeds further north and west, there are twenty-one other Communes between the lower course of the Gironde and the Bay of Biscay, with vineyards which are capable of producing 16,700 *tonneaux* of wine, mostly red wine, each year. None of the wines of the "Médoc" vineyards is of outstanding excellence, and the only *Appellation Contrôlée* to which they are entitled is plain *Médoc*. There are wines of this part of the Bordeaux country, however, which are distinctly better than the rest, owing to the greater care given both to the growing of the grapes and the making of the wine. Such are the wines of the following Châteaux:

Du Castéra (Private Society): 150 *tonneaux* red and 125 *tonneaux* white wines.

Laujac (Cruse Fils Frères): 50 *tonneaux* red wine.

Livran (James Denman & Co.): 150 *tonneaux* red and 50 *tonneaux* white wines.

Loudenne (W. & A. Gilbey & Co.): 125 *tonneaux* red wine.

Château Saint-Brice and *Château Bégadan-Médoc* are registered labels used, the first for the wines of the *Cave Co-opérative de Saint-Yzans*, and the second for those of the *Cave Co-opérative de Bégadan*.

Bourg and Blaye

Across the broad waters of the Gironde, facing the Médoc, the vineyards of Bourg and Blaye produce an average of 73,000 *tonneaux* of red and white wines of which about 5,500 *tonneaux* are red wines of fair quality, the peers of the *Crus Bourgeois du Médoc*, whilst 31,000 *tonneaux* are more ordinary red wines, and 36,500 *tonneaux* are white wines, most acceptable wines, of course, but not remarkable. None but the better wines of both Bourg and Blaye vineyards are entitled to be sold either as *Côtes de Bourg* or *Premières Côtes de Blaye*, provided their strength is not inferior to 10°.5 of alcohol.

In the Bourg district, the more highly prized wines are those from Châteaux du Bosquet, Tayac, Falfas and Rousset. Another favourite is Château Mille Secousses, a showplace of some 250 acres, mostly alongside the right bank of the Gironde.

In the Blayais, the more highly prized wines are those of Châteaux Charron and La Barre, in the Parish of Saint-Martin; Château Bellevue, at Plassac; Châteaux Saugeron, Le Cone Taillasson and Cap-de-Haut, at Blaye; Château Les Alberts, at Mazion; Château Les Fours, at Fours; and Château La Tour-Gayet, at Saint-Androny.

To the east of Bourg and Blaye, the vineyards of the Cubzac district – or Cubzagais – produce an average of 5,000 *tonneaux* of red wines and 3,500 *tonneaux* of white wines every year, none better-known than those of Château de Terrefort, the average yield of its vineyards being 300 *tonneaux* of red and 30 *tonneaux* of white wines. The red wines of the Cubzagais are entitled to the *Appellation Contrôlée* "Bordeaux" when their strength is not less than 9°.75 of alcohol, and "Bordeaux Supérieur" when their alcoholic strength reaches 10°. The white wines of the Cubzagais can only claim to be "Bordeaux Blanc" when they reach 10°.5 and "Bordeaux Blanc Supérieur" with an 11°.5 alcoholic strength.

The Garonne

The Garonne is one of the great rivers of France, as every Frenchman knows, and the finest river in the world to all true *Bordelais*. The Garonne rises at the foot of the Maladetta, the highest of the mountains of the Pyrenées range, and it flows in a north-westerly direction through the Départements of the Haute-Garonne, Tarn-et-Garonne, and Lot-et-Garonne, before entering the Département of La Gironde, which it crosses until it reaches Bordeaux, where it ceases to be a very ordinary river, in no way different from many other quite ordinary rivers. It develops greater width and depth, real majesty and grace, at the same time as taking upon itself the very modern air and activity of a busy rendezvous of the merchant seamen of the world. Some 15 miles from Bordeaux, the Garonne meets the Dordogne, when both rivers lose their identity and become the Gironde.

During the whole of its course through the Département of the Gironde, with the exception of its passage through Bordeaux, the Garonne flows through vinelands many of which produce some of the best and most famous of all red and white table wines, wines which may well be divided into three main sections: (1) Graves; (2) Sauternes and Barsac; (3) Cérons, Loupiac and Premières Côtes de Bordeaux.

Graves

The vineyards of the district known as Les Graves or Graves de Bordeaux, on account of their gravelly soil or subsoil, are dotted here and there along the left bank of the Garonne for some 12½ miles in length and 5 miles in width, from Blanquefort southwards.

The Graves vineyards produce a greater quantity of red wines, or Claret, than white wines, in spite of the unshakeable belief throughout the English-speaking world that a *Vin de Graves* invariably means a white wine. What is of much greater importance is the fact that a fair proportion of the red Graves wines, of which the average annual production is over 9,000 *tonneaux*, are wines of very high quality, some of them the peers of the finest red wines of the Médoc, whereas only a very small proportion of the white wines of Graves, of which the average annual production is below 6,000 *tonneaux*, have any claim to rank among the great table wines such as the best white wines of the Rhine or Burgundy.

According to the ruling of the *Appellations contrôlées* authorities, there are two qualities of *Vins de Graves*, depending upon their alcoholic strength: plain *Graves*, if their alcoholic strength is not less than 10° but under 12°; and *Graves Supérieures*, when their alcoholic strength reaches 12° or is higher than 12°. Besides their alcoholic strength, both *Graves* and *Graves Supérieures*, whether red or white, must be wines from grapes grown within the boundaries of one or the other of the only thirty-six Communes recognised as belonging to the *Graves de Bordeaux* district. A list of these Communes, given in alphabetical order for the sake of quicker reference, follows. Their geographical position will be seen on the map of *Les Graves* at the end of the book.

Appellation d'Origine Contrôlée "Graves"

Crus classés by the Institut National des Appellations d'Origine

RED WINES	WHITE WINES
CADAUJAC: Château Bouscaut.	CADAUJAC: Château Bouscaut.
LEOGNAN: Ch. Haut-Bailly, Ch. Carbonnieux, Dom. de Chevalier, Ch. Malartic-Lagravrière, Ch. Olivier, Ch. de Fieuzal.	LEOGNAN: Ch. Carbonnieux, Ch. Chevalier, Ch. Olivier, Ch. Malartic-Lagravière.
MARTILLAC: Ch. La Tour, Ch. Smith-Haut-Lafitte.	TALENCE: Château La Ville-Haut-Brion.
PESSAC: Ch. Haut-Brion, Ch. Pape Clément.	VILLENAVE D'ORNON: Château Couhins.
	MARTILLAC: Château La Tour.

Communes of "Les Graves"

	Optimum output per annum in tonneaux			Optimum output per annum in tonneaux	
	RED WINE	WHITE WINE		RED WINE	WHITE WINE
Arbanats	250	300	Mérignac	70	–
Aiguemorte-les-Graves	250	50	*Pessac	350	8
*Beautiran	550	35	Portets	1,700	100
*Bègles	30	–	Pujols-sur-Ciron	–	650
Budos	100	200	Roaillan	50	250
Cabanac-Villagrains	25	100	Saint-Médard d'Eyrans	85	100
*Cadaujac	500	60	Saint-Michel de Rieufret	20	10
Canejan	50	–	Saint-Morillon	40	400
Castres	200	180	Saint-Pardon	40	30
Cestas	35	–	Saint-Pierre de Mons (or		
Eysines	250	–	St-Pey de Langon)	150	500
*Gradignan	150	25	Saint-Selve	120	350
Isle Saint-Georges	1,350	–	Saucats	70	100
La Brède	250	250	*Talence	150	15
Landiras	150	450	Toulenne	100	200
Langon	200	450	*Villenave d'Ornon	600	15
Léogeats	50	50	Virelade	200	250
*Léognan	600	330			
*Martillac	350	70		9,185	5,728
Mazères	100	200			

(* indicates Communes producing the best Graves wines.)

(a) Red Wines

The wines of Graves have not been officially graded as the red wines of the Médoc and the white wines of Sauternes were "classified" in 1855. The only red Graves which was included in the 1855 "Classification" was Château Haut-Brion, which was given a place among the *Premiers Crus Classés* of the Médoc, Lafite, Latour and Margaux.

The production of red wines of the Graves vineyards is much smaller than that of the vineyards of the Haut-Médoc, and the proportion of fine wines is also smaller, probably not more than 11% of the total, which represents roughly 1,000 *tonneaux* of red wines comparable in quality to those of the *Crus Classés*, *Crus Exceptionnels* and *Crus Bourgeois Supérieurs* of the Haut-Médoc.

No Château of the Médoc has a more illustrious lineage or a finer wine tradition than Château Haut-Brion. It was bought in 1837 by a Monsieur Larrieu, in whose family it remained until 1922. Under what may be called the Larrieu dynasty, the red wine of Haut-Brion was second to none and often the best of all. All who had, as I had, the privilege of enjoying the Haut-Brion 1864, 1865, 1868, 1874 and, above all, 1871 and 1875, and later 1893, 1899, 1900, and 1906, can never forget their exquisite delicacy and charm; there never was any better red table wine. Then came the tragedy of a change of ownership. M. André Gibert bought Haut-Brion in 1922, and the Haut-Brion 1923 was the last great Haut-Brion for twenty years! It was during this unhappy period that white grapes were planted at Haut-Brion and there has been ever since a white Haut-Brion, just one more white Graves wine, a wine that has no faults and no real appeal, neither sweet nor dry, quite good, of course, but not great.

Happily, Haut-Brion has now new masters, with both the resources and the will to make again wines really worthy of the proud name of Haut-Brion.

In the following list, first place has been given to the half-dozen Graves wines which I happen to like best, and then, in alphabetical order, the names of two dozen of the better-known Châteaux of the Graves de Bordeaux, producing red wines, ranging from fair to very fine in quality:

Châteaux	Optimum output per annum in tonneaux
Château Haut-Brion, *Pessac*	150
Domaine de Chevalier, *Léognan*	30
Château Haut-Bailly, *Léognan*	60
Château La Mission-Haut-Brion, *Talence*	80
Château Pape Clément, *Pessac*	100
Château Smith-Haut-Lafitte, *Martillac*	200

Châteaux	*in Tonneaux*
Château Baret, *Villenave d'Ornon*	18
Château Bouscaut, *Cadaujac*	100
Château Carbonnieux, *Léognan*	80
Château-Neuf, *Léognan*	20
Château de Hilde, *Bègles*	70
Château Des Carmes-Haut-Brion, *Pessac*	15
Château Fieuzal, *Léognan*	30
Château La Garde, *Martillac*	100
Château La Louvière, *Léognan*	85
Château Larrivet-Haut-Brion, *Léognan*	30
Château La Tour Haut-Brion, *Talence*	18
Château La Tour Martillac et Kresmann-La-Tour, *Martillac*	40
Château Le Pape, *Léognan*	15
Château Malartic-Lagravière, *Léognan*	50
Château Olivier, *Léognan*	20
Château Poumey, *Gradignan*	20
Château du Tuquet, *Beautiran*	75
Château Valoux, *Cadaujac*	18

(b) White Wines

The white wines of the Graves vineyards are of two sorts, the dry and the sweet; the dry wines being only fairly dry, never possessing the so clean finish of a genuine Chablis, for instance, and the sweet wines only fairly sweet, lighter of body, but not nearly so luscious as any of the fine Sauternes. Many of the white Graves are very pleasing wines indeed, but they are not endowed with any great character or outstanding personality which would make it possible even if it were fair to sell them at anything like the same prices as an Yquem or a Montrachet. The difference between good wines and great wines is that the first must of necessity be good value to be acceptable, whereas the great wines are so rare and so good that their cost does not matter so much, as there are always a few people who must have them, cost what they may. There are great wines among the red Graves, but not among the white, which belong, even the best of them, to the category of "good" wines. All "good" wines should be reasonably priced that they may be enjoyed by the many sensible people who, be they rich or not, expect to have their money's worth. This is why the majority of the white Graves are not sold under the name of the vineyard or the date or vintage of their birth, but under a registered trade mark and undated. They are mostly blends of white wines from different Graves vineyards, as well as of different years, the better wines of the better years bringing up the standard of quality of the wines of the less favoured vintages. The Bordeaux shippers responsible for such blends are thus able to offer white Graves of the same type and quality year after year, and at much the same price, irrespective of ups and downs – mostly ups – of market quotations.

There are, however, many dry white Graves which are sold under the names of their individual vineyards; they possess greater individuality and, when made in a good vintage year, they are distinctly superior as well as dearer than the blends. Here is a list of some of such white Graves, a small list selected on account of their greater popularity, sometimes the recognition of finer quality and sometimes also the reward of abler salesmanship.

Châteaux	*Optimum output per annum in Tonneaux*
Château Baret, *Villenave d'Ornon*	20
Château Bouscaut, *Cadaujac*	20
Château Cantebau-Couhins, *Villenave d'Ornon*	10
Château Carbonnieux, *Léognan*	80
Château Chevalier, *Léognan*	15
Château Couhins, *Villenave d'Ornon*	30
Domaine de Grandmaison, *Léognan*	5
Château de la Brède, *La Brède*	16
Château de Respide, *St. Pierre de Mons*	100
Château Ferran, *Martillac*	10
Château Ferrande, *Castres*	50
Château Fieuzal, *Léognan*	15

Châteaux	Optimum output per annum in Tonneaux
Château Haut-Nouchet, *Martillac*	10
Château La Tour, *Léognan*	10
Château La Tour Martillac et Kressmann-La-Tour, *Martillac*	15
Château La Ville Haut-Brion, *Talence*	22
Château Le Désert, *Léognan*	10
Château Le Pape, *Léognan*	10
Château Malleprat, *Martillac*	15
Château Olivier, *Léognan*	100
Château Poumey, *Gradignan*	10
Château du Tuquet, *Beautiran*	75
Château Virelade, *Arbanats*	10

Sauternes and Barsac

Sauternes is the name given to one of the greatest white wines of the world by one of the smallest of the Communes or parishes of the Gironde Département, some 20 miles to the south of Bordeaux, four miles west of the Garonne, beyond Barsac and the little river Ciron.

Sauternes is a sweet white wine, different from and superior to other sweet white wines. It is made from white grapes grown in the vineyards of the Commune of Sauternes and from those of the four adjoining Communes of Bommes, Barsac, Preignac and Fargues. The excellence and characteristic features of the white wines known as Sauternes are due in the first place to the nature of the soil and subsoil of those five Communes, and in the second to the manner in which the grapes are picked at the vintage time, and pressed. When the Sauternes grapes are ripe, they are not picked but allowed to "rot", and although theirs may be a "noble rot", *la pourriture noble*, it is none the less a form of rot which is brought about by a peculiar mould known as *botrytis cinerea*, a parasite which, like all parasites, lives at the expense of its host. Its fine rootlets pierce the tender golden skin of the ripe grapes, thirsting for the moisture within: the grapes lose their shape and colour, as their juice loses some of its water, hence the greater proportion of sugar to water which is responsible for the sweetness of the wine eventually. Besides this greater concentration of grape sugar, the intervention of the *botrytis cinerea* is responsible for quite minute yet most important changes in the constitution of the grape-juice, and it is to these changes that the wines of Sauternes owe, besides their sweetness, their characteristic individuality.

The *botrytis cinerea* settles upon the Sauternes grapes when they are ripe, but in so haphazard a fashion, that, at the vintage time, there are in every bunch of grapes some "sound" golden berries, which have so far been overlooked by the *botrytis;* others covered with a dust of spores, which have got a hold but are not yet at work; whilst some berries, those upon which the *botrytis* settled first and has got busy, are shrunk and shrivelled, brown and unappetizing. They are the best, the "nobly rotten" berries, more rotten than noble to look at, but the only ones that the long, sharp-pointed scissors of the pickers will seek and cut off. During the next six or seven weeks, according to the weather, the same pickers will return to the same bunches in search of any more berries which may have become fit for the press. In the end, when fogs and frosts are threatening, all bunches are picked, whatever the condition may be of the few berries left on them, but the wine which is pressed from them is kept apart; it is very different from the *Tête de Cuvée*, that is the wine made from the pickings of chosen over-ripe grapes.

Barsac is one of the more important and one of the best-known Communes of the Gironde Département. It lies between the Garonne, to the east, and its tributary, the Ciron, to the south; with the Graves country both to the north and west. Its vineyards produce very large quantities of fairly sweet white wines, probably more than half of those that are sold as plain "Sauternes", besides those sold as "Barsac". This is because Barsac has long been wedded to Sauternes, on the other side of the Ciron, but has not given up its own or maiden name; it is thus legally entitled to sell under either name the less distinguished of its wines. "Haut-Barsac" is the name given to blends of white wines from those vineyards of the Barsac Commune which are farther away from the Garonne. Of course, all the finer wines of Barsac always bear the name of the Château or Estate of their birth, and although they may look just the same as the anonymous blends, their *bouquet*, flavour, breed and appeal are altogether different.

In 1855, when the best wines of the Médoc were graded in five classes, the best white wines of the five Sauternes Communes were also graded in First and Second Growths, with Château d'Yquem in a class by itself ahead of the First Growths. The *Premiers* and the *Deuxièmes Crus Classés de Sauternes*, and their average production of white wines, are distributed among the five Communes of Sauternes, Bommes, Barsac, Preignac and Fargues, as follows:

Châteaux	Optimum output per annum in Tonneaux
SAUTERNES	
Château d'Yquem, *Premier Grand Cru*	100
Château Guiraud, *Premier Cru*	80
Château Filhot, *Deuxième Cru*	50
Château d'Arche, *Deuxième Cru*	25
Château Lamothe, *Deuxième Cru*	25
Château d'Arche-Lafaurie, *Deuxième Cru*	35
Château Lamothe-Bergey, *Deuxième Cru*	20
Crus Bourgeois Supérieurs	75
Crus Bourgeois et Bons Artisans	100
	510
BOMMES	
Château La Tour Blanche, *Premier Cru*	90
Château Lafaurie-Peyraguey, *Premier Cru*	60
Château de Rayne-Vigneau, *Premier Cru*	100
Château Rabaud, *Premier Cru*	75
Cru Haut-Peyraguey, *Premier Cru*	30
Crus Bourgeois Supérieurs	80
Crus Bourgeois et Artisans Supérieurs	15
	450
BARSAC	
Château Coutet, *Premier Cru*	60
Château Climens, *Premier Cru*	45
Château Doisy-Védrines, *Deuxième Cru*	80
Château Doisy-Daëne, *Deuxième Cru*	20
Château Doisy-Dubroca, *Deuxième Cru*	50
Château Myrat, *Deuxième Cru*	50
Château Broustet, *Deuxième Cru*	30
Château Caillou, *Deuxième Cru*	50
Château Suau, *Deuxième Cru*	15
Château Nairac, *Deuxième Cru*	25
Crus Bourgeois Supérieurs	713
Crus Bourgeois et Crus Artisans	350
	1,488

Plate 5 CLARET GRAPE. The *Cabernet franc*. One of the grapes principally responsible for the individuality and excellence of the red wines of Bordeaux, particularly in the Médoc.

Châteaux	*Tonneaux*
PREIGNAC	
Château de Suduiraut, *Premier Cru*	100
Château de Malle, *Deuxième Cru*	40
Crus Bourgeois Supérieurs	720
Crus Bourgeois et Crus Artisans	250
	1,110
FARGUES	
Château Rieussec, *Premier Cru*	100
Château Romer, *Deuxième Cru*	15
Crus Bourgeois et Artisans	150
	265
Total:	3,783 *tonneaux*

Some 1½ miles to the east-north-east of Sauternes, the Commune of Saint-Pierre-de-Mons, also known as Saint-Pey-de-Langon, half a mile to the east of Langon, on the left bank of the river Garonne, produces some quite ordinary red wines and about 500 *tonneaux* per annum of very fair white wines, some of them not unlike the white wines of Sauternes, although the only *Appellation Contrôlée* to which they are entitled is that of "Graves Supérieures". The best Estate of this Commune is Château de Respide, with an average annual production of 100 *tonneaux* of good white wines.

Cérons, Loupiac and Premières Côtes de Bordeaux

There are many other vineyards in the Valley of the Garonne, above Bordeaux, which produce a fair quantity of red wines, which are by no means remarkable, and a great deal more white wines of much greater merit.

On the left bank of the Garonne, 22 miles south of Bordeaux, immediately north of Barsac, there are three Communes which occupy a small plateau and are called Cérons, Podensac and Illats. Their vineyards produce on an average 200 *tonneaux* of white wines, some of them fairly dry, more like the white Graves wines, and others distinctly sweet, more like those of nearby Barsac, and all of them are entitled to the *Appellation Contrôlée* "Cérons". Château de Cérons et Calvimont is one of the finest estates of this district.

Plate 6 A CLARET GRAPE. *The Merlot.* Another of the grapes grown in the Gironde, together with the Cabernets, for making the red wine of Bordeaux. It is particularly suited to the soil of the St Emilion and Pomerol districts.
These grapes were actually photographed at Château Ausone, where it is claimed that wine has been made without interruption since Roman days.

On the right bank of the Garonne, 27 miles s.s.e. of Bordeaux, facing Langon and the Sauternes country beyond, the Commune of Sainte-Croix-du-Mont produces both red and white wines, but it is chiefly noted for the high quality of its rich white wines, the annual production of which reaches 1,500 *tonneaux*. The more renowned of the vineyards of Sainte-Croix-du-Mont are the Châteaux de Taste, Loubens, Lamarque, Lafue, La Mouleyre and Laurette.

Loupiac, immediately to the north of Sainte-Croix-du-Mont, facing Barsac on the other side of the Garonne, produces some 1,200 *tonneaux* of very fair white wines per annum, as well as a good deal of undistinguished red wines. None but the better white wines of Loupiac are entitled to the *Appellation Contrôlée* "Loupiac". The finest Estate of Loupiac is Château de Ricaud, with an average annual production of 125 *tonneaux* of good white wines.

Premières Côtes de Bordeaux is an *Appellation Contrôlée* to which are entitled both the red and the white wines from the vineyards of 34 other Communes of the right bank of the Garonne, from Bordeaux to Verdelais, Saint-Maixant, Gabarnac and Saint-Germain-de-Grave, nearly 33 miles s.s.e. of Bordeaux. Their vineyards produce on an average 16,000 *tonneaux* of red wines and 17,000 *tonneaux* of white wines per annum.

The Dordogne

The Dordogne is one of the fairest of the great rivers of France. It owes its name to two small rivers of the Mont Dore, La Dore and La Dogne, which meet and flow together in a westerly direction for some 300 miles, never for long out of sight of some vineyards, until they reach the Bec d'Ambès, where they join the Garonne and become the Gironde. During nearly half its course, the Dordogne meanders in a lazy fashion across the Gironde *Département*, with the many vineyards of Saint-Emilion and Pomerol to its right, and the even more numerous vineyards of the Entre-deux-Mers to the left, that is mostly southwards.

The two more important cities on the Dordogne within the boundaries of the Gironde Département are Libourne and Castillon. Libourne, at the junction of the Dordogne and L'Isle, is, after Bordeaux, the most important wine mart of the Gironde Département. It was a flourishing town, called Caudate, during the Roman occupation, and it was rebuilt in 1286 by Edward I's *Sénéchal*, Roger Leyburn, whose name it bears to this day. Castillon, a busy and pleasant little market town today, used to be one of the chief military outposts of Guyenne and it was there that Talbot was defeated and killed in 1453.

Between the two rivers the Dordogne and the Isle, there is a cluster of vine-clad hills, and it is on top of one of these, the one that is nearest to Libourne, that the quaint old city of Saint-Emilion is perched. Its steep cobbled streets, its sun-tanned gabled houses, and its ruined cloisters huddle around its very ancient and truly remarkable monolith church, hewn out of the living rock, over which was built some centuries later the great spire that is such a landmark for many miles.

Saint-Emilion

The wines of Saint-Emilion are all red wines, deep, dark, true red, not blood-red, and without any trace of mauve or tawny twilight in their bright purple. The greatest wines of Saint-Emilion are the peers of the greatest Médoc and Graves Clarets, but there are very few of them. The great majority of the wines of Saint-Emilion may not have the distinction or "breed" of the great Médoc wines; they may lack something of the suave charm of the greatest red Graves wines, but they possess in an exceptional degree such obvious plain honest-to-God goodness, that we immediately welcome them as friends that will never let us down or lay us low.

Besides the vineyards of the Commune of Saint-Emilion itself, those of five other Communes, immediately to the north, west, east and south of the quaint old city of Saint-Emilion, produce large quantities of red wines which are entitled to the *Appellation Contrôlée* "Saint-Emilion". All the best wines, however, are known as *"Premiers Crus"*, and they come from named vineyards of the Saint-Emilion Commune. Locally, as well as among the Bordeaux merchants, there is a distinction made between the wines from those vineyards which are closer to the city of Saint-Emilion, and the others which are half-way on the road to Pomerol: the first are called *Vins de Côtes*: they are upon higher and more stony ground; the others are called *Vins de Graves*: they are upon the lower, more gravelly and deeper soil.

We may well wonder why the 1855 Classification completely ignores the great wines of Saint-Emilion and Pomerol, the Ausone, Cheval Blanc and Petrus to name but three whose good vintages fetch in the open market prices just as high as, and often higher than, those paid for most classed growths of the Médoc. And it is likewise rather puzzling to find Haut-Brion among the First Growths but no other red Graves deemed worthy to be placed in any of the other four groups. The answer is that the red wines of Graves, Saint-Emilion and Pomerol were not enjoying, a hundred years ago, anything like the popularity which we consider to be their due today. There cannot be any doubt of this lack of appreciation since the prices paid at the time for the wines of Graves and Saint-Emilion – there was no mention of Pomerol – are a mere fraction of the prices paid for those of the Médoc. I do not believe that there was ever anything like a corresponding difference in the quality of the wines themselves. If the wines of Graves and Saint-Emilion were in such poor demand during the first half of the last century that the Bordeaux brokers ignored them completely in 1855, and if those same wines are today enjoying a vogue far greater than they did only fifty years ago, I am inclined to blame fickle fashion. The soil of the vineyards and their grapes have been the same all the time, so that there cannot have been such an extraordinary change in the quality of the wines. They must have been grossly underrated in the past, and many of them are certainly overrated, or at any rate over-priced, today. Here is a list of the highest prices paid *de première main* before 1855:

(Prices given are in francs for Tonneaux)

	1825	1830	1835	1840	1844
Premiers Crus	5,000	2,400	1,600	2,500	4,500
Deuxièmes Crus	4,200	2,000	1,200	1,100	2,800
Troisièmes Crus	2,400	1,400	1,000	850	2,400
Quatrièmes Crus	1,800	900	800	700	1,800
Cinquièmes Crus	1,100	700	600	550	1,300
Bourgeois Supérieurs	800	500	350	450	900
Petits Bourgeois	600	400	280	280	600
Bas Médoc	450	550	200	180	350
Graves	1,200	500	450	400	700
Saint-Emilion	800	600	250	350	600
Palus	550	400	180	230	300
Côtes	380	350	150	180	260

(Wm. Franck: *Traité sur les Vins du Médoc, troisième édition;* Bordeaux. 1853.)

In the following pages the best growths of Saint-Emilion have been listed separately as *Vins de Côtes* and *Vins de Graves*. The names with two asterisks are those of the *Premiers Grands Crus Classés* and those with one are those of the *Grands Crus Classés*, according to the official Classification of the 16th June, 1955, by the Institut National des Appellations d'Origine.

Saint-Emilion — Vins de Côtes

Châteaux	Optimum output per annum in Tonneaux
PREMIER GRAND CRU	
**Château Ausone	25
PREMIERS CRUS	
*Clos de l'Angélus	130
Château Baleau	80
*Château Balestard-La-Tonnelle	60
Château Beau-Mazérat	20
**Château Beauséjour (Duffau-Lagarosse)	25
**Château Beauséjour (Dr. Fagouet)	40
**Château Belair	40
*Château Bellevue	30
*Château Bergat	15
Château Berliquet	35
Château Bragard	40
*Château Cadet-Bon	25
Château Cadet-Peychez	5
*Château Cadet-Piola	20
**Château Canon	75
*Château Canon-La-Gaffelière	100
Château Cantenac	40
*Château Cap-de-Mourlin	75
Château Cardinal-Villemaurine	40
Château Cassevert	20
*Château Chapelle-Madeleine	30
Château Côte-Daugay-ex-Madeleine	12
*Château Coutet	50
*Château Curé-Bon-La-Madeleine	25
*Château Faurie-de-Soutard	50
*Château Fonplégade	50
**Clos Fourtet	60
*Château Franc-Mayne	30
Château Franc-Pourret	35
Domaine du Grand-Faurie	20
*Château Grand-Mayne	60
*Château Grand-Pontet	50

Châteaux	*Tonneaux*
*Château Grandes Murailles	10
*Château Guadet-Saint-Julien	16
Château Gueyrot	41
Château Haut-Cadet	25
Château Haut-Pontet	25
Château Haut-Simard	30
Château Haut-Trimoulet	10
*Clos des Jacobins	40
*Château La Carte	35
*Château La Clotte	16
Château La Clotte-Grande-Côte	10
*Château La Clusière	15
*Château La Couspaude	30
Château La Fleur	40
**Château La Gaffelière-Naudes	100
*Clos La Madeleine	10
Clos de la Magdeleine	6
Château Laniote	30
*Château Larmande	45
*Château Laroze	100
Château l'Arrosée	50
*Château La Serre	35
Château La Tour-du-Guetteur	3
Château La Tour-Saint-Emilion	10
*Château Le Couvent	5
*Château Le Prieuré-Saint-Emilion	16
Château l'Hermitage de Mazérat	30
**Château Magdelaine	20
Château Magnan-La-Gaffelière	40
Château Malineau	20
Château Matras	35
*Château Mauvezin	20
*Château Moulin-du-Cadet	20
Château Moulin-Saint-Georges	55
**Château Pavie	150
*Château Pavie-Decesse	40
*Château Pavie-Macquin	60
*Château Pavillon-Cadet	25

Châteaux	*Tonneaux*
*Château Petit-Faurie-de-Soutard	80
*Château Saint-Georges-Côte-Pavie	25
*Clos Saint-Martin	20
*Château Sansonnet	35
Château Simard	100
Clos Simard	5
*Château Soutard	60
Château Soutard-Cadet	10
*Château Tertre-Daugay	30
*Château Trimoulet	60
*Château Trois-Moulins	15
*Château Troplong-Mondot	125
**Château Trottevieille	50
Clos Valentin	15
Château Vieux-Moulin-du-Cadet	10
*Château Villemaurine	70
Average total production of the Premiers Crus de Saint-Emilion (Côtes)	3,432
Average total production of the other vineyards of Saint-Emilion (Côtes)	1,960
	5,392

Saint-Emilion — Vins de Graves

PREMIER GRAND CRU

*Château Cheval Blanc	100

PREMIERS CRUS

**Château Chauvin	60
*Château Corbin	100
*Château Corbin-Michotte	50
Château Cormey-Figeac	45
*Château Croque-Michotte	60
**Château Figeac	100
*Château Grand-Barrail-Lamarzelle-Figeac	120
Château Grand-Corbin	50
*Château Grand-Corbin-Despagne	100
*Château Jean-Faure	80

Châteaux	Tonneaux
*Château La Dominique	60
*Château La Marzelle	25
*Château La Tour-du-Pin-Figeac (Bélivier)	50
*Château La Tour-du-Pin-Figeac (Moueix)	50
*Château La Tour-Figeac	80
Château Monlabert	50
*Château Ripeau	50
Château Vieux-Château-Chauvin	20
*Château Yon-Figeac	90
Average total production of the *Premiers Crus de Saint-Emilion* (Graves)	1,270
Average total production of the other vineyards of Saint-Emilion (Graves)	726
	1,996

Communes entitled to sell their Wines with the Appellation "Saint-Emilion"

Communes	Tonneaux
Saint-Christophe-des-Bardes	1,550
Saint-Etienne-de-Lisse	1,850
Saint-Hippolyte	1,100
Saint-Laurent-des-Combes [1]	700
Saint-Pey-d'Armens	600
Saint-Sulpice-de-Faleyrens	1,350
Vignonet	1,100
	8,250

[1] The finest Estate of this Commune, Château Larcis-Ducasse, has been given the *Appellation contrôlée* 'Saint-Emilion Grand Cru Classé'.

Communes Producing Red Wines similar to those of Saint-Emilion

Saint-Georges:	*Appellation contrôlée* "Saint-Georges-Saint-Emilion"	1,100
Montagne:	*Appellation contrôlée* "Montagne-Saint-Emilion"	3,200
Lussac:	*Appellation contrôlée* "Lussac-Saint-Emilion"	2,550
Puisseguin:	*Appellation contrôlée* "Puisseguin-Saint-Emilion"	2,750
Parsac:	*Appellation contrôlée* "Parsac-Saint-Emilion"	500
Libourne:	*Appellation contrôlée* "Sables-de-Saint-Emilion"	350
		10,450

Total Production of Saint-Emilion Wines

Communes	Tonneaux
Commune de Saint-Emilion	6,300
Communes entitled to the *Appellation* "Saint-Emilion"	8,250
All other Communes	10,450
Grand Total	25,000

Pomerol

Immediately to the west of the Graves de Saint-Emilion, north-east of Libourne, the vineyards of Pomerol occupy a plateau of some 1,800 acres and produce some 1,500 *tonneaux* of very good red wines, the peers of the *Premiers Crus* of Saint-Emilion, practically the same in colour and body but possessing a very charming and characteristic *bouquet* of their own. Some of them are also somewhat softer and more gracious than their Saint-Emilion first cousins.

Premiers Crus de Pomerol

Châteaux	*Tonneaux*
Château Beauregard	65
Clos Beauregard	50
Château Bourgneuf	50
Château Certan	20
Château Certan-Marzelle	20
Château Clinet	30
Clos du Clocher	20
Château Feytit-Clinet	25
Château Gazin	80
Château Gombaude-Guillet	25
Château Grate-Cap	30
Château Guillot	30
Château Haut-Maillet	17
Château La Cabanne	60
Château La Commanderie	20
Château La Conseillante	40
Château La Croix	50
Château La Croix-de-Gay	20
Château La Croix-Saint-Georges	20
Château Lafleur	16
Château La Fleur-Pétrus	35
Château Lagrange	20
Château La Grave-Trigant-de-Boisset	25
Clos de la Gravette	10
Château de La Nouvelle-Eglise	10
Château La Pointe	70
Château Le Caillou	30
Château Le Gay	25
Clos L'Eglise	25
Domaine de l'Eglise	20
Château l'Eglise-Clinet	20
Château l'Enclos	40
Château l'Evangile	45
Château Moulinet	40

Châteaux	*Tonneaux*
Château Nénin	100
Château Petit-Village	60
Château Petrus	25
Château Plince	40
Château Rouget	80
Clos du Roy	15
Château de Sales	180
Château Taillefer	50
Clos des Templiers	20
Château Trotanoy	30
Vieux Château Certan	50
Château Vraye-Croix-de-Gay	15
	1,668
Other vineyards of the Commune of Pomerol	815
	2,483

The Communes of Néac and Lalande-de-Pomerol, which adjoin the Commune of Pomerol, have a great many vineyards which produce on an average 2,200 *tonneaux* of very fair red wines, which are sold under the *Appellations Contrôlées* 'Néac' and 'Lalande-de-Pomerol'.

The Fronsadais

The Fronsadais is the name given to the most extensive as well as the most picturesque of the Dordogne vinelands within the Département of the Gironde. It is named after its chief city, the little port of Fronsac, some two miles to the north-west of Libourne, facing south, and the river Dordogne, and with the valley of the river Isle as its eastern boundary.

The best wines of the Fronsadais are those of the many vineyards which crowd the slopes of the range of hills nearest to the Dordogne, and parallel to it, known as *Côtes de Canon-Fronsac:* none but the red wines of those vineyards are entitled to the *Appellation Contrôlée* "Côtes de Fronsac", and all of them are within the boundaries of one or the other of the twin Communes of Fronsac and Saint-Hippolyte-de-Fronsac. Their total annual yield is not more than 1,200 *tonneaux*, 700 from Fronsac and 500 from Saint-Hippolyte vineyards.

Immediately behind this first range of hills, there are others which stand guard

over them to the north and north-west, and their steeper slopes are also thickly
planted in vines, partly in the same Communes of Fronsac and Saint-Hippolyte-
de-Fronsac, but mostly on the territory of the four adjoining Communes of La
Rivière, Saint-Germain-La-Rivière, Saint-Aignan, and Saillans. Their average
annual yield is 3,500 *tonneaux* of very fair red wines which are entitled to the
Appellation Contrôlée "Côtes de Fronsac". On the whole, the Côtes de Fronsac
wines may not have the "breed" or elegance which one associates with all the
best wines of Saint-Emilion and Pomerol, but some of them, those of Château
Rouet in particular, the most important as well as the finest estate of the Commune of Saint-Germain-La-Rivière, are the peers of many better-known, and
also more expensive wines of other Dordogne vineyards.

The bulk of the wines of the Fronsadais, however, are plain *ordinaires* with no
other claim than to the name of "Bordeaux" or – the best of them – "Bordeaux
Supérieur". They are produced by the vineyards of a number of Communes
along a somewhat uneven plateau occupying the central and northern parts of
the *Canton de Fronsac*. The names of those Communes and their average production per annum of both red and white wines, in tonneaux, are as follows:

COMMUNES	RED WINES	WHITE WINES	TOTALS
Asques	1,300	–	1,300
Cadillac-en-Fronsadais	500	300	800
Galgon	500	1,500	2,000
Lalande-de-Fronsac	300	500	800
Lugon et L'Ile-du-Carney	2,500	500	3,000
Mouillac	100	200	300
Périssac	200	800	1,000
Saint-Genès-de-Fronsac	–	1,200	1,200
Saint-Romain-la-Virvée	1,200	–	1,200
Vérac	300	600	900
Villegouge	800	600	1,400
	7,700	6,200	13,900

The total wine production of the Fronsadais is about 22,000 *tonneaux* per annum, divided as follows:

	Tonneaux
Côtes de Canon Fronsac (Red Wines)	1,200
Côtes de Fronsac (Red Wines)	3,500
Bordeaux and *Bordeaux Supérieurs* (Red and White)	13,900
Palus wines from riverside vineyards of La Dordogne and L'Isle	3,300
	21,900

Beyond the Fronsadais, but still within the Département of the Gironde, the Cantons of Guitres and Coutras have a very large number of vineyards which are responsible for an annual production of some 21,000 *tonneaux* of *ordinaires* wines, 5,000 of red wine and 16,000 of white.

Entre-Deux-Mers

The name Entre-deux-Mers is given to the largest of the wine-producing areas of the Gironde Département, all the land that lies between the rivers Garonne and Dordogne until they meet and become the Gironde. There are some 76,000 *tonneaux* of red and white wines produced every year by the vineyards of the Entre-deux-Mers, mostly white wines and mostly ranging from "*très ordinaires*" to "*ordinaires*" and "*bons ordinaires*". The white wines of the Entre-deux-Mers vineyards are entitled to the *Appellation Contrôlée* "Entre-deux-Mers" or "Bordeaux" when their alcoholic strength is not less than 10°, and they are entitled to the *Appellation Contrôlée* "Bordeaux Supérieur" when their alcoholic strength is not less than 11.5°. Red wines are entitled to the *Appellation Contrôlée* "Bordeaux" when their alcoholic strength is not inferior to 9.75°, and "Bordeaux Supérieur" when it is 10° or over.

DÉPARTEMENTS DE LA GIRONDE

Optimum output per annum in tonneaux

GIRONDE	RED WINES	WHITE WINES	TOTALS	
Médoc	45,000	1,500	46,500	
Bourgeais et Blayais	36,500	36,500	73,000	119,500
GARONNE				
Graves de Bordeaux	9,000	6,000	15,000	
Sauternes, Barsac, Cérons et Sainte-Croix-du-Mont	–	6,500	6,500	
Premières Côtes de Bordeaux	16,000	17,000	33,000	
Côtes de Bordeaux-Saint-Macaire	3,500	5,500	9,000	
Bazadais	500	500	1,000	64,500
DORDOGNE				
Saint-Emilion	25,000	–	25,000	
Pomerol	2,500	–	2,500	
Néac & Lalande-de-Pomerol	2,000	–	2,000	
Fronsadais	20,000	2,000	22,000	
Cantons de Guîtres et Coutras	5,000	16,000	21,000	
Cubzagais	5,000	3,500	8,500	
Graves de Vaires	3,000	1,000	4,000	
Sainte-Foy-de-Bordeaux	4,000	7,500	11,500	96,500
ENTRE-DEUX-MERS	26,000	50,000	76,000	76,000
	203,000	153,500	356,500	356,500

CHAPTER THREE

The Wines of Burgundy

BURGUNDY IS THE NAME of one of the old Provinces of France which was cut up, at the time of the French Revolution, into three Départements: the Yonne, in the north; the Côte d'Or, in the centre; and the Saône-et-Loire, in the south.

Burgundy is also the name of the wine made from grapes grown in the vineyards of Burgundy, most of it red wine, but much of it white. Both the red and white wines of Burgundy are the only wines of France possessing such superlative excellence that they can and do challenge the wines of Bordeaux as the greatest table wines of the world.

In colour and alcoholic strength, most red wines of Burgundy, when unfortified or otherwise tampered with, are not unlike most red wines of Bordeaux, but they differ from them in *bouquet*, flavour, appeal and personality. They rarely possess quite the same light and delicate texture or body which is such an outstanding character of most fine Clarets; they are as a rule more robust, more assertive, more immediately obvious, which is why there is a great number of people, more particularly among the young, who prefer Burgundy to Bordeaux. The difference between them is not one of "quality" but of "tone", just as the voice of a soprano differs from that of a contralto, not necessarily in quality but inevitably in tone. We may prefer one to the other or we may, and I certainly do, love them both equally.

It is not quite the same, however, as regards the white wines of Burgundy. None of them is comparable to the fine luscious white wines of Sauternes, but most of them are wines of more distinctive and of finer quality than the other table wines of the Gironde, the Loire, the Rhône, the Rhine or anywhere else in France. There are, of course, many charming, light, white wines from other parts of France which are quite as good as the lighter white Burgundies of the Yonne and Saône-et-Loire Départements, but they do not possess the breed, body, *bouquet* and balance of the great white wines of the Côte d'Or.

The quality and the personality of the wines of Burgundy, be they red or white, are due primarily to the geological formation of their vineyards, that is to the nature of both soil and subsoil; this varies, of course, from place to place, but not from year to year. Wherever it happens to be best, mostly upon the lower half of the hillsides, the wine will be best; wherever it is too poor or too

Plate 7 SAUTERNES. The name given to one of the greatest white table wines in the world by one of the smallest Communes or Parishes of the Bordeaux country. The mellow and luscious quality of Sauternes makes it the ideal wine to drink with fruit or sweets. The glass shown is of a shape favoured by the wine shippers of Bordeaux as being both graceful and helpful to bring out the *bouquet* in the wine.

cold, as it usually is on hilltops, the grapes will not ripen properly; and when it is too heavy and too rich, as it always is in plains and vales, the vines will give an abundance of grapes from which none but the commoner types of wine are made. The soil is a gift; it must be received gratefully and used as best we can, but it cannot be changed. Besides the soil of the vineyards, climatic conditions have also a great deal to do with the quality of the wine. Like the soil, rain and sunshine are gifts which we must accept as and when they come. Unlike the soil, however, climatic conditions are never quite the same from year to year, and they have the greatest share of responsibility in the differences of quality that exist between the wines made by the same man, from grapes grown in the same vineyard, in different years. Last, but by no means least, the quality and person-ality of the wines of Burgundy are due in a very large measure to the species of grapes from which they are made. This, of course, is entirely a matter of choice. Since grapes have been grown and wine has been made in Burgundy for over a thousand years, we can surely take it for granted that the grapes now being grown have been selected as best suited to both the soil and climate of Burgundy. All the great red and white wines of Burgundy are made from noble Pinot grapes. The red wines are made mostly from the *Pinot noir fin* or *Pinot noirien;* also, to a very much smaller extent, from two of its first cousins, the *Pinot Beurot* and the *Pinot Liebault;* all the best white wines are made almost exclusively from *Pinot Chardonnay;* also, in a very minor degree, from its first cousin, *Pinot Blanc.*

But all Burgundy wines are not great wines. There are many more good wines than great ones, particularly in the more southern vinelands of Burgundy; the Mâconnais and Beaujolais. Most of the plainer *ordinaires* red wines of Burgundy are made from *Gamay noir à jus blanc*, and a small quantity from both this black Gamay with the white juice and its poor relation, the *Gamay à jus coloré*. The *Appellations Contrôlées* authorities insist that the proportion of this commoner Gamay with red juice must not exceed 10% of the total vines in any one vine-yard. As regards the more *ordinaires* white wines of Burgundy, there are but two species of grapes from which they are made; the one which is grown mostly is the *Aligoté;* the other is the *Gamay blanc*, also known as *Melon.*

In Burgundy, a wine-producing village, parish or area, is known as *Finage*, and the site of any vineyard within the bounds or limits of each *Finage* is known as *Climat*. The best wines from the best *Climats* of each *Finage* are known as *Têtes de Cuvée;* the next best are called *Premières Cuvées*, and the next *Deuxièmes* and *Troisièmes Cuvées*, that is wines of the first, second and third class.

The making of red and white table wines in Burgundy rests on exactly the same basic principles as everywhere else. The grapes are picked when they are fully ripe, but not overripe; they are usually *égrappées*, that is, freed from their

Plate 8 A SAUTERNES GRAPE. The *Sémillon*. These bunches are of small, white, overripe, wrinkled grapes, affected by the *pourriture noble*, the fungus which is responsible for the unique sweetness and richness of the white wines of Sauternes and Barsac. This photograph was taken at Château Filhot.

stalks in an *égrappoir*, a kind of rotating callender-barrel made for the purpose. The berries burst as they are torn from their stalks; their sweet juice runs and is collected as *vin de goutte* in wooden vats; then the deflated but still very moist grapes are pressed hard and they give up all the remaining juice that was in them, which is what they call the *vin de presse*. Both the *vin de goutte* and the *vin de presse*, either separately or after being mixed together, start fermenting in the open vats and cast off any dirt that may have come in with the grapes from the vineyards; a few days later, when their first bout of fermenting fever is over, the quieter newly-born wines are lodged in casks, with the bung out or loose, so that any carbonic acid gas generated during the slower but still continuous process of fermentation may escape.

Chaptalisation is the addition of sugar to the grapes before they are pressed, in order to raise the sugar content of the new wine, hence also its alcoholic strength after fermentation; it is practised in Burgundy to a greater extent than in Bordeaux, because unsatisfactory vintages, when the grapes do not get all the sunshine and heat that they need, are more frequent in the Côte d'Or than in the Gironde. It is also due, however, to the fact that there is now a majority of wine drinkers, and more particularly throughout the English-speaking world, who have acquired somehow the conviction that a red Burgundy is a wine more than halfway from Bordeaux to Oporto. Curiously enough, there was a time, during the nineteenth century, when one could see some white Chardonnay grapes growing in all the greatest red Burgundy vineyards. The demand was at the time for "elegant" Burgundies, and it was considered that the blending of a little white Pinot wine with the red gave to the wine the lighter touch or "elegance" that was demanded then.

The sugaring of wine in the making, or *Chaptalisation*, is permitted by French law within certain limits, of course, but the mixing of Burgundy with other wines, from the Midi, Algeria, Spain or anywhere else, can only be done at the cost of the loss of the name *Bourgogne*. The *Appellations Contrôlées* law, which is strictly applied in France but has, of course, no claim to any jurisdiction outside France, does not allow any wine to be offered for sale under a geographical name other than that of its birthplace. Of course, it is only right, but at the same time it adds a great deal to the problems which many an honest Burgundy shipper must face, handicapped as no other is by the fact that the best vineyards of Burgundy are so small and so much divided among different owners; it makes it exceedingly difficult to secure adequate supplies of fine wines, more particularly those bearing popular names, which are in much greater demand than all others. This is why the practice of the Champagne Shippers for the past hundred years has been adopted by most Burgundy Shippers, and is rapidly spreading. That is, to ignore names of Communes and vineyards, and to make blends to be sold under merchants, names or trade marks, averaging quality and cost, and building up adequate supplies to meet the demand. Such blends are usually very good value and some of them are also quite fine wines. The name and reputation of the Shipper are, of course, all-important.

Chablis

Chablis is a charming little town in the topmost corner of the Yonne Département, a little more than half-way between Paris (183 km. to the north) and Dijon (134 km. to the south).

Chablis has given its name to one of the most attractive dry white wines in the world, a wine that is pale gold in colour, free from sweetness and acidity alike, intensely "clean" on the palate, light yet by no means weak, not assertive and not possessive but still less dull or flat. Chablis is the most universally welcome partner for fish, oysters, and also for all sorts of white meat.

Unfortunately, the deserved popularity of Chablis is responsible for the fact that the demand all over the world is far greater than the supply of genuine Chablis, that is, the wine made from grapes grown upon the gentle slopes of a few hills in the valley of the small river Serein, within the bounds of the Commune of Chablis, and of a few other nearby Communes, from Pontigny, in the north, to Poilly-sur-Serein in the south; and from Viviers, near Tonnerre, in the east, to Chitry and Saint-Bris, near Auxerre, in the west. Even within this comparatively small area there are marked differences in the quality of the wines from various vineyards, and the authorities responsible for the *Appellations Contrôlées* have decreed that Chablis shall be sold, at any rate in France, under four different labels, according to the standard of excellence of the wines of four categories of Chablis vineyards, to be known as:

(1) *Chablis Grand Cru* or *Grands Chablis;* (2) *Chablis Premier Cru;* (3) *Chablis;*
(4) *Petit Chablis* or *Bourgogne des Environs de Chablis.*

(1) Chablis Grand Cru or Grands Chablis

A wine may not bear either of these names unless it complies with the following conditions:

(a) it must be made from Pinot grapes exclusively;

(b) and from the best of the named vineyards of the Communes of Chablis, Milly and Poinchy;

(c) its alcoholic strength must not be inferior to 11°;

(d) the vineyard which produced the grapes from which the wine was made must not yield more than 35 hectolitres (770 gallons) per hectare, or about 310 gallons per acre. This official limiting of the yield is the official recognition that quantity is never attained except at the expense of quality.

(2) Chablis Premier Cru

To be allowed to use this name, followed by the name of an individual vineyard, a wine must comply with the following conditions:

(a) it must be made from Pinot grapes exclusively,

(b) and from any of the "next best" vineyards of the same three Communes of Chablis, Milly and Poinchy;

(c) the alcoholic strength must not be inferior to 10.5°;

(d) the yield must not have exceeded 40 hectolitres of wine (880 gallons) per hectare, or about 360 gallons per acre.

(3) Chablis

The conditions required for the use of the plain or unqualified name of Chablis are as follows:

(a) the wine must be made from Pinot grapes exclusively;

(b) and from the vineyards of any of the twenty *Communes chablisiennes*, or Communes of the Chablis district, i.e., Beines, Béru, Chablis, Chemilly-sur-Serein, Chichée, Courgis, Fleys, Fontenay, Fyé, La Chapelle, Ligny-le-Chatel, Lignorelles, Maligny, Milly, Poilly, Poinchy, Préhy, Rameau, Villy, Viviers;

(c) the alcoholic strength of the wine must not be inferior to 10°.

(4) Petit Chablis or Bourgogne des Environs de Chablis

These names are given to the more *ordinaires* white wines of the Chablis district, and the only conditions attached to their use is that the wines that bear them will have:

(a) been made from any species of grapes other than *producteurs directs* – the ungrafted vine briars;

(b) that such grapes shall have been grown in any of the twenty *Communes chablisiennes;*

(c) that the alcoholic strength shall not be below 9.5°.

Chablis Vineyards

The best Chablis vineyards, those which are responsible for the *Crands Chablis* or *Chablis Grand Cru,* are those which one sees as one leaves Chablis by the road leading to the north-east, upon the slopes of the hill rising from the right bank of the river Serein. The five best are Blanchots, Les Clos, Valmur, Grenouilles and Vaudésir. Then come Preuses and La Moutonne [1]; a little to the north, Vaulorent, Bougros and Fourchaume; also, to the south, Chapelot, Montée de Tonnerre and Mont de Milieu.

There are in the three favoured Communes of Chablis, Milly and Poinchy, a number of less famous vineyards, to the west and north-west of Chablis itself, responsible for many fair and fine wines which are not likely to reach the high standard of excellence of the wines from the vineyards upon the right bank of the river Serein, but they cost less and may be as good or better value. There are fourteen of these "*deuxièmes crus*", as follows:

Beauroy, Beugnon, Butteaux, Châtin, Côte de Fontenay, Côte de Léchet, Les Forêts, Les Lys, Melinots, Montmain, Pied d'Aloup, Roncières, Séchet, Troëme, Vaillon, Vaucoupin and Vaupinent.

The Côte D'Or

The Côte d'Or is the name of a French Département, not one of the greatest, but one of the more illustrious in the annals of military history, piety and gastronomy. Dijon, its metropolis, was for centuries the capital city of the great

---

[1] La Moutonne is the name of a small vineyard of 128 *ares,* or about 3 acres and one sixth, wedged between the Preuze and Vaudésir vineyards, but the name, which was registered as a trade mark, became widely known through judicious publicity. According to a ruling of the French Courts in 1951, however, the name of La Moutonne may no longer be used – in France – for any other white wine except that of the small La Moutonne vineyard.

warring Ducs de Bourgogne. It was also the birthplace of Saint Bernard, and the Abbey of Clairvaux is not far away. The vineyards of the Côte d'Or still bring forth, as they have done for over a thousand years, wines of superlative excellence to partner the fine fare from local farms, orchards and open country.

The Côte d'Or owes its name to the apparently inexhaustible gold mine of its vineyards, or so we are told by some authorities, but, according to others, it was so called on account of the "cloth of gold" which it puts on in the autumn, when the woods of the hilltops and the vineyards of the hillsides are a riot of colour and a true "slope of gold". It is made up of a broken chain of vine-clad hills of which there are two main groups, the Côte de Nuits, to the north, from below Dijon to below Nuits-Saint-Georges, with some 3,000 acres of first-class vineyards; and the Côte de Beaune, to the south, from above Beaune to below Santenay, with some 7,000 acres of first- and second-class vineyards. The whole length of both these groups of gentle hills is about 38 miles, and the background of both is high mountainous country known as *Arrières-Côtes* or *Hautes-Côtes*.

All the better vineyards of the Côte d'Or are planted upon the lower slopes of the hills, facing east, the rising sun and the sombre Vosges beyond; or south-east and south, facing the fir-clad Monts Jura not very far away and the snow-capped Alps in the distance. There are also vineyards upon the higher ground of the Hautes-Côtes, immediately behind the Côte itself, as well as in front of it, in the great plain that stretches as far as the Saône, but they do not produce any wines comparable to those of the Pinot-planted vineyards of the Côte: their grapes are mostly Gamay for the red wines and Aligoté, for the whites, commoner, hardier and also more generous species of grapes than the noble Pinots.

The Pinot-planted hillside vineyards of the Côte d'Or cover barely 10,000 acres and their vines do not give more than 27.5 gallons of wine per acre, on an average, which means a maximum production of 2,750,000 gallons of really fine red and white wines, or 1,375,000 dozens of fine Burgundy, not a large quantity considering that, besides the local demand, there are so many wine lovers throughout the civilised world who would very much like to drink genuine Burgundy, if only they knew where to find it.

The figures given represent the approximate "optimum" production of the more important vineyards in *Queues*, the Burgundian term for two *Pièces*, or 456 litres, very nearly equal to 100 gallons. It must be borne in mind that "optimum" figures are very different from "average" figures: they represent the maximum yield of wine not only obtainable but also permitted by the *Appellations Contrôlées* authorities of 275 gallons per acre. Unfortunately, there are frost-bitten springs and rain-soaked summers when the vineyards do not bring forth more than half, or even less, their "optimum" or maximum.

Fixin

Coming from Dijon, Fixin is the first village we come to where they make fine wine. There was a time when the wines of Chenôve, Marsannay-la-Côte, and Couchey, three villages between Dijon and Fixin, enjoyed a fair measure of favour, but they have now fallen by the way. All Fixin wines are red, from fair to fine, with one great wine, the *Clos de la Perrière*.

		Queues (100 gallons)
	Tête de Cuvée	
Clos de la Perrière		34
	Premières Cuvées	
Les Arvelets		24
Clos du Chapitre		33
Aux Cheusots		13
Les Hervelets		33
Les Meix-Bas		3.75
All others		56.25
	Total	163 *queues*
Deuxièmes Cuvées		31
Troisièmes Cuvées		90
	Total	121 *queues*
	Grand Total	318 *queues*

Brochon

A Commune which is chiefly known locally for its inexpensive, *ordinaires* Gamay-grown red wines, but there are also about a hundred acres of Pinots-growing vineyards which are capable of producing 220 *Queues* of red wine entitled to the *Appellation Contrôlée Vins fins de la Côte de Nuits*.

Gevrey-Chambertin

Gevrey appears for the first time in the annals of Burgundy in A.D. 895, when the village was presented to the Abbey of Saint-Benigne, but it was only in 1847 that it hyphenated its name with that of its most famous vineyard, Chambertin (32 acres). Chambertin, as a vineyard, dates from the 13th century, but the *Clos de Bèze* (37 acres), which it adjoins, was planted in A.D. 630 by the monks of the Abbaye de Bèze. The wines of both vineyards are the only ones entitled to the illustrious name of Chambertin, Napoleon's favourite wine. Wines, however, made from grapes grown in the *Clos de Bèze* part of the vineyard, may be, and are often sold as *Chambertin-Clos de Bèze*. Seven of the *Premières Cuvées* of Gevrey-Chambertin may also add the name of Chambertin to their own.

	Queues (100 *gallons*)
Têtes de Cuvée	
Chambertin and Clos de Bèze-Chambertin	176
Premières Cuvées	
Chapelle-Chambertin	56
Charmes-Chambertin	88
Griotte-Chambertin	18
Latricières-Chambertin	49
Mazys-Chambertin	61
Mazoyères-Chambertin	103
Ruchottes-Chambertin	24
Cazetiers	57
Clos Saint-Jacques	49
Etournelles	14
Fouchère	7
Varoilles	42
	568 *queues*
Deuxièmes Cuvées	162
Troisièmes Cuvées	556
	718

Grand Total 1,462 *queues*

There is no *Grand Chambertin* any more than *Petit Chambertin* in the Côte d'Or and a wine named *Grand Chambertin* in a wine-merchant's price-list or on an hotel wine-list may or may not be genuine and quite good, but it is wrongly described.

There are red Burgundies as good as a good Chambertin but none better. Unfortunately, the 70 acres of Chambertin-cum-Clos de Bèze vineyard belong to a number of people, all of whom have not got the same skill, means or pride, which is why two bottles of Chambertin may be equally genuine without being equally good, let alone great. It is also why it is of such importance, when buying Burgundy, to find out whenever possible the name of the *vigneron* who made it or of the merchant who selected it. This does not apply to Chambertin alone, but to all the vineyards of Burgundy which are owned by a number of different proprietors.

Another remark which applies not only to Gevrey-Chambertin but to all the other Communes which have added to their original name that of their more famous vineyard, like Vosne-Romanée, Chambolle-Musigny, Nuits-Saint-Georges, etc., is that the first name is the one that really counts. A Gevrey-Chambertin is one of the plain or *ordinaires* wines of Gevrey without a drop of Chambertin in it; had it any claim to genteel birth, it would give the name of the vineyard of its birth, such as Latricières-Chambertin or Clos Saint-Jacques.

Morey-Saint-Denis

Morey, the next village we come to as we leave Gevrey, is much older. It dates from the Gallo-Roman period, but it was only on the 19th January, 1927, that Morey added to its name that of one of its smallest vineyards, the Clos Saint-Denis. Its two largest and more illustrious vineyards are the Clos de Tart and the Clos des Lambrays. Both owe their well-deserved reputation to the fact that they are the property each of a single owner. Clos de Tart belongs to M. Jean Mommessin and the Clos des Lambrays, formerly the property of M. Camille Rodier, now belongs to Madame Cosson. Both vineyards produce well-balanced, full-bodied red wines which deserve and reward long keeping, and single ownership means that one can be sure that all bottles bearing the same name and date are really the same wine. This cannot be said of the *Bonnes Mares* vineyard, a small part of which is on Morey soil whilst much the greater part is in the adjoining Chambolle territory. *Bonnes Mares* can be, and should be, a softer and rather more gracious wine, but here again there are different owners, hence differences in the wines that bear and are entitled to bear the same name.

In Morey-Saint-Denis they also make some small quantity of very pleasing white wine.

	Queues (100 gallons)	
Têtes de Cuvée		
Bonnes Mares	12	
Clos de Tart	49	
Clos des Lambrays	61	
Clos de la Roche	32	
Clos Saint-Denis	15	
	169	*queues*
Premières Cuvées		
Calouère	9	
Chabiots	15	
Chaffots	9	
Charmes	9	
Charnières	17	
Chenevery	25	
Chéseaux	18	
Côte Rôtie	4	
Faconnières	12	
Fremières	16.5	
Froichots	4.5	
Maison Brulée	13	
Meix-Rentier	8	
Millandes	30	
Mochamps	18	
Monts-Luisants	22	
Morey	22.5	
Ormes, Clos des	31.5	
Sorbet, Clos	24	
	308	*queues*
Deuxièmes Cuvées	154	
Troisièmes Cuvées	106	
	260	
Grand Total	737	*queues*

Chambolle-Musigny

Immediately south of Morey we come to Chambolle, once upon a time a Roman camp, and now one of the more prosperous communities of the Côte d'Or. It was in 1875 that Chambolle added to its name that of its most illustrious vineyard, Musigny. The two best vineyards of Chambolle-Musigny are *Bonnes Mares*, in the north, where it adjoins Morey-Saint-Denis, and Musigny, in the south, where it adjoins Flagey-Echézeaux. *Musigny* is one of the most exquisite of the great red table wines of the world, whether *Grand Musigny* or *Petit Musigny*. The Musigny vineyard is cut in two by a small country road, the larger half being locally known as Grand Musigny and the smaller half as Petit Musigny, but there is no difference whatever in the quality of the wine. Beyond the municipal boundary of Chambolle-Musigny, another vineyard which is really the continuation of Musigny, but is in the adjoining Commune of Flagey-Echézeaux, is known as La Combe d'Orveau, but its wines are so good that they are allowed to be sold under the noble name of Musigny. There is a small quantity of white Musigny made in all good vintages: it is made of noble Chardonnay grapes and it is a fine wine although it cannot ever claim to be as great a wine as the red. The Musigny vineyards are shared among a few proprietors, all of them anxious to make better wine than anybody else. The Comte de Vogüé owns the greatest share of the Musigny vineyards.

	Queues (100 gallons)		*Queues* (100 gallons)
Têtes de Cuvée			
Les Musigny	66	Gruenchers	23
Les Bonnes Mares	90	Haute-Doix	14
	———	Lavrottes	8
	156 *queues*	Noirots	22
		Senticrs	38
Premières Cuvées			———
Amoureuses	41		342 *queues*
Baudes	27		
Charmes	45	*Deuxièmes Cuvées*	600
Combe d'Orveau	39	*Troisièmes Cuvées*	216
Cras	32		———
Derrière la Grange	5		816
Fuées	48	Grand Total	1,314 *queues*

Vougeot

Vougeot is a modest little village: it owes its name to a small stream, the Vouge, which comes out of the hillside above Chambolle-Musigny and rushes down towards the plain through Gilly-les-Vougeot. The original village of Gilly, after adding to its own name that of its one vineyard, the finest of the Côte d'Or, *Clos Vougeot*, has now practically dropped the "Gilly" altogether: it is now nearly always referred to as Vougeot, *tout court*.

The Clos Vougeot or *Clos de Vougeot*, as it was originally called and is still called to-day occasionally, was planted centuries ago by the monks of Citeaux and its 125 acres were surrounded by a high wall that enclosed it, hence its name of Clos. Much of the original wall still stands, but a number of entrances have been cut in it by some of the owners: there are fifty-four of them, of whom but two own a substantial share of the famous Clos. M. J. Morin, has nearly 14 acres, and Madame Veuve Noëllat, nearly 6 acres. There are four other proprietors who own 5 acres, more or less; they are M. Louis Gros, Messrs. Champy Père et Fils, M. P. Misset and M. G. Grivot. The other forty-odd owners have a few vines only, but the little wine that they make is nevertheless genuine *Clos de Vougeot*. This makes it very difficult, however, to pass judgement upon the wines of so large a vineyard which has been broken up into so many small fractions. In the days of single monastic ownership, there were three separate wines or *Cuvées* made each year. The best was the wine made from the grapes from the higher part of the vineyard, farthest from the road and close to the Château, where the monks had their wine-press and *cellier;* the second best wine was made from grapes half-way between the road and the *cellier,* and *cuverie;* and the third best was made from grapes from the lower part of the vineyard, those nearest the main road from Paris to Rome on its Dijon-Beaune lap.

There is a small country road which leads from the village to the Château, now the headquarters of the Confrérie des Chevaliers du Tastevin. At the Château end of this road, there is a small vineyard of some 5 acres, "La vigne blanche", which is entirely planted with white Chardonnay grapes. It is owned by L'Héritier-Guyot, who make the white wine known as *Clos Blanc de Vougeot*

Flagey-Echézeaux

Flagey, immediately south of Gilly-les-Vougeot, to the west of the Route Nationale, added the name of its more famous vineyard to its own, in 1886. Its best vineyards produce red wines which are the peers of the very best, and one can hardly be surprised since they enjoy the same kind of soil, altitude and aspect as the vineyards of Chambolle-Musigny, to the north, Vosne-Romanée, to the south, and the Clos Vougeot to the west.

	Queues (100 gallons)
Têtes de Cuvée	
Les Grands Echézeaux	60
Les Echézeaux du Dessus	24
	84 *queues*
Premières Cuvées	
Beaux-Monts-Bas	42
Champs-Traversins	28
Cruots ou Vignes Blanches	25
Loachausses	29
Orveau, En	75
Poulaillères	40
Quartiers de Nuits	21
Rouges-du-Bas	31
Saint-Denis, Clos	14
Treux, Les	38
	343 *queues*
Deuxièmes Cuvées	50
Troisièmes Cuvées	77
	127 *queues*
Grand Total	554 *queues*

Pinots-grape wines from unspecified Flagey-Echézeaux vineyards may be sold under the better-known name of the nearby Commune of Vosne-Romanée.

Vosne-Romanée

Vosne is a tight little island of stone houses in a sea of Pinots. Its vineyards stretch from those of Flagey-Echézeaux to the north to those of Nuits-Saint-Georges to the south, mostly between the village and the Route Nationale. The best vineyards of Vosne-Romanée, however, are all upon the other or west side of the village, upon the lower slopes of the Côte.

	Queues (100 gallons)		Queues (100 gallons)
Têtes de Cuvée		Malconsorts	46
Romanée Conti	11	Petits-Monts, Aux	16
La Romanée	5.5	Reignots, Aux	13
La Tâche	9.5	Romanée-Saint-Vivant	73
Les Richebourg	33	Suchots	101
Les Varoilles [1]	20		
	79 *queues*		353 *queues*
Premières Cuvées		*Deuxièmes Cuvées*	308
Beaux-Monts	19	*Troisièmes Cuvées*	524
Brulées, Aux	30		832 *queues*
Gaudichots	45		
Grande-Rue	10	Grand Total	1,264 *queues*

Romanée Conti is usually given first place among the Romanées, but there has been more than one occasion when I would have given the palm to La Tâche or to Richebourg, which is a Romanée under another name. There is no doubt that the Romanée-Richebourg wines are among the greatest of all red wines: they are the peers of Chambertin, Musigny, and Clos Vougeot, with, of course, a personality entirely their own. Their *bouquet* has a spicy sweetness that is almost oriental, and there is in the texture of their body a caressing quality which is quite wonderful.

Romanée Conti and La Romanée are owned the first by M. de Vilaine and the second by Messrs. Liger-Belair. M. de Vilaine is the chairman of the *Domaine de la Romanée Conti*, a syndicate who own besides the Romanée Conti vineyard, the whole of La Tâche, and important parts of Richebourg and Grands-Echézeaux. Until the second world war, the *Domaine de la Romanée Conti* managed to save many, if not most, of its old French vines, but the last of these had to be done away with soon after the end of the war. The Romanée Conti vineyard has now been replanted with French Pinots noiriens, grafted on bug-resisting American briars, and it is hoped that in due course these new vines will produce wines which may be worthy of the proud name that will be theirs.

[1]   The wine of Les Varoilles is sold under the name of Richebourg.

Nuits-Saint-Georges

Nuits-Saint-Georges is no village but a very much alive little town, with some 3,000 inhabitants, probably more than half of them members of well-to-do *vignerons* and wine-merchant families. Nuits-Saint-Georges is the principal market-town and shopping centre of the Côte de Nuits, 13 miles south of Dijon and 10 miles north of Beaune. It was only in 1892 that Nuits added to its name that of its best vineyard, Saint-Georges. The reputation of the Saint-Georges vineyard dates back to A.D. 1023 when this vineyard was given to the Canons of Saint-Denis. The vineyards of Nuits-Saint-Georges and those of the adjoining Commune of Prémeaux, which has been granted the privilege to sell its wines under the name of Nuits-Saint-Georges, are of much greater extent than those of the other Communes of the Côte de Nuits, and they produce more wine than any of them. All the red wines of Nuits-Saint-Georges are somewhat stout of body but by no means ungainly, the best of them, particularly the Saint-Georges and Vaucrains, are bigger than a Musigny or Richebourg of the same age, but by no means heavy: they may not be as great as these, but they are certainly very good wines, always dependable, hence eminently satisfactory.

	Queues (100 gallons)
Têtes de Cuvée	
Le Saint Georges	58
Boudots	49
Cailles	29
Cras	24
Murgers	37
Porrets	54
Pruliers	55
Thorey & Clos de Thorey	48
Vaucrains	42
	396 *queues*
Premières Cuvées	
Château-Gris	16
Chaboeufs	22
Chaignots	43
Perrières et Clos des Perrières	23
Poulettes	16
Procès	14

	Queues (100 gallons)
Richemonnes	16
Roncières	15
Rue de Chaux	24
	189 *queues*
Deuxièmes Cuvées	1,100
Troisièmes Cuvées	440
	1,540 *queues*
Grand Total	2,125 *queues*

All the *climats* of Nuits-Saint-Georges are shared by different owners, except Les Porrets, the property of M. H. Gouges, and Château Gris, the property of Messrs Lupé-Cholet, an outstanding wine which well deserves a place among the *Têtes de Cuvée*.

Prémeaux

This village dates back to the Roman occupation but it does not appear to have ever hit the headlines in the course of the centuries. Its vineyards produce wines of the same character and excellence as those of Nuits-Saint-Georges, which they adjoin, their only particular distinction being that one of Prémeaux's *Premières Cuvées*, Clos Arlot, produces the only Nuits-Saint-Georges white wine.

	Queues (100 gallons)
Têtes de Cuvée	
Didiers-Saint-Georges	22
Clos des Forêts-Saint-Georges	39
Corvées	60
Corvées-Pagets	18
	139 *queues*
Premières Cuvées	220
Deuxièmes Cuvées	177
	397 *queues*
Grand Total	536 *queues*

Plate 9 BURGUNDY. The *Vignoble* at Aloxe-Corton. This picture typifies the gentle slopes of the Côte d'Or just north of Beaune at Aloxe-Corton, whence come some of the great Burgundies. The best vineyards lie to the west of the main Beaune-Dijon road. They are very small in extent and do not compare in size or output with the larger Châteaux of the Médoc.

After Nuits-Saint-Georges and Prémeaux, the best vineyards of the Côte de Nuits come to an end. There are three small Communes, Prissey, Comblanchien and Corgoloin, which produce a small quantity of red wines and a much smaller quantity of white wines, none of them of outstanding merit but some of them good enough to be entitled to the *Appellation Contrôlée* "Vins fins de la Côte de Nuits".

Côte de Beaune: Aloxe-Corton

We then come to the Côte de Beaune, with the village of Aloxe which added to its name that of its best *climat*, Corton, in 1862. It nestles among its vineyards upon a steep hill of its own, the top of which is thickly wooded. There are some 500 acres of first-class vineyards within the administrative limits of the Aloxe-Corton Commune, mostly facing south or south-east and producing both red and white wines of very high quality. The best red wine of Aloxe-Corton is *Le Corton*, and many claim that it is the best red wine of the Côte de Beaune. The best white wine is made from Chardonnay grapes from the largest vineyard of Aloxe-Corton, called *Charlemagne* in memory of the great Emperor of the West who did much to encourage viticulture.

	Queues (100 gallons)		Queues (100) gallons
Têtes de Cuvée		Les Grèves	14
Le Corton	88	Les Meix-Lallemant	14
En Charlemagne	132	Les Perrières	5
Clos-du-Roi	81	La Vigne-au-Saint	83
Les Chaumes	29	Other *Premières Cuvées*	18
Les Renardes	116		
			299 *queues*
	446 *queues*		
Premières Cuvées		**Deuxièmes Cuvées**	352
		Troisièmes Cuvées	253
Les Bressandes	131		
Les Chaumes-de-la-			605 *queues*
Voirosse	24		
Les Fiètres	10	Grand Total	1,350 *queues*

There are two other villages, one below and the other above Aloxe-Corton, the best wines of which are entitled to be sold under the name of Corton. The first is Ladoix-Serrigny, which is cut in two by the Route Nationale 74 from Dijon to Beaune: its Pinot-planted vineyards cover about 75 acres and the three best of them, locally known as Vergesses-Corton, Le Rognet-Corton and Clos des Corton-Faiveley, have an optimum production of 77 *queues* or 7,700 gallons

Plate 10 A Sauternes Grape. *The Sauvignon blanc.* Another noble white grape, grown and used with the Sémillon, to make the best wines of Sauternes. The bunches are not cut off at vintage time, but they are looked over, week after week, and none but the ripest berries are picked each time. This photograph was taken at Château d'Yquem.

of very good red wines, of the same standard of excellence as those of nearby Aloxe-Corton. The other village, to the n.n.w. of Aloxe-Corton, upon the other side of the same hill, is Pernand, which has added to its name that of its best vineyard, Les Vergelesses, and is now called Pernand-Vergelesses. Its only *Tête de Cuvée* is Ile des Vergelesses, with an optimum production of 66 *queues*, or 6,600 gallons, of fine quality wine. The best red and white wines of Pernand may be sold as *Corton* or *Aloxe-Corton* (the reds), and *Charlemagne* and *Corton-Charlemagne* (the whites).

Savigny-les-Beaune

South of Pernand and north of Beaune, there are about 1,000 acres of vineyards: they are those of Savigny-les-Beaune, a straggling village clinging to both banks of the little river Rhoin, at the opening of the pretty Fontaine-Froide vale. The vineyards of Savigny stretch as far west as the Route Nationale 74, but those responsible for the best wines, all of them red wines, are the hillside vineyards both north, next to those of Pernand, and south, next to the Beaune vineyards.

	Queues (100 *gallons*)			*Queues* (100 *gallons*)
Têtes de Cuvée			*Premières Cuvées*	1,030
Les Vergelesses	131		*Deuxièmes Cuvées*	282
Les Marconnets	72		*Troisièmes Cuvées*	711
Les Jarrons	70			2,023 *queues*
	273 *queues*		Grand Total	2,296 *queues*

Beaune

Beaune, about half-way between Dijon and Chalon-sur-Saône, is a very ancient walled city of the greatest possible interest. Whether it is actually the Bibracta of Caesar's *Commentaries* or not is for historians to settle, but there cannot be any doubt about its importance as the metropolis of the Burgundian vinelands, and the age-long fame of its own vineyards. Many were praised by name centuries before any other vineyards of France – the Clos de la Mousse, in 1220, when it was bequeathed to the Chapter of Notre-Dame de Beaune; Les Marconnely, in 1256; Les Cras, in 1303; Les Grèves, in 1343; Les Fèves, in 1483; and so on. Carthusians, Benedictines and the Knights of Malta were for centuries among the largest of the Beaune vineyard owners, but today their vineyards are shared by many different proprietors. *Les Grèves*, for instance, the largest of the *climats* or vineyards of Beaune, nearly 80 acres, upon the lower slopes of the Mont Battois, produces some of the best red wines of the Côte de

Beaune but by no means all of the same high standard: that which is made from the top corner of the vineyard, the property of the Carmelites of Beaune until 1789 and now owned by Messrs Bouchard Père et Fils, is of quite outstanding excellence. This particular corner of the Grèves vineyard was named by the Carmelites *La Vigne de l'Enfant-Jésus,* and its wines have been sold under that name ever since: it was named after the arms of Beaune which represent the Blessed Virgin standing with the "Enfant Jésus" upon her left arm, and in His right hand, a vine branch with a bunch of grapes.

Têtes de Cuvée	*Queues* (100 *gallons*)		*Queues* (100 *gallons*)
Clos-de-la-Mousse	26	*Premières Cuvées*	2,222
Clos-des-Mouches	170	*Deuxièmes Cuvées*	562
Les Bressandes	143	*Troisièmes Cuvées*	440
Les Champimonts	128		3,224 *queues*
Les Cras	39		
Les Fèves	33	Grand Total	4,086 *queues*
Les Grèves	245		
Les Marconnets	78		
	862 *queues*		

In that part of the Clos des Mouches, which belongs to M. Joseph Drouhin, Chardonnay grapes have been planted and a good white wine is made.

Hospices de Beaune

In Beaune there are churches, quaint old houses, remains of the old city walls, great cellars, and other tokens of the city's ancient fame as well of its civic and commercial activities today. But the pride of Beaune is Les Hospices de Beaune. There is nothing like it anywhere else in the world. Five hundred years of devoted service to relieve the sufferings of the poor is a fine record, but it may not be unique in the annals of charity. What is unique is the exquisite beauty of the Hôtel-Dieu which Nicolas Rolin built in 1443, and the fact that the ever rising cost of its upkeep has been met from the time of its founder's death until today by the wine made from the vineyards bequeathed to the Hospices, first of all by Nicolas Rolin and his widow, Guigone de Salins, and ever since by other benefactors. The vineyards belonging to the Hospices de Beaune are scattered all along the Côte de Beaune, from Aloxe-Corton to Meursault, and the Hospices wines are sold every year by public auction on the third Sunday in November under the names of 29 different Cuvées, most of them bearing names of benefactors, mostly the names of donors of the vineyards belonging to the Hospices.

Hospices de Beaune

Finage or Village	Cuvées
RED WINES	
Aloxe-Corton	Charlotte Dumay
	Dr Peste
Savigny-les-Beaune	Du Bay-Peste-Cyrot
	Forneret
	Fouquerand
Beaune	Nicolas Rolin
	Guigone de Salins
	Dames hospitalières
	Estienne
	Brunet
	Hugues et Louis Bétault
	Rousseau-Deslandes
Pommard	Dames de la Charité
	Billardet
Volnay	Blondeau
Monthelie	Jacques Lebelin
	Henri Gélicot
Auxey-Duresses	Boillot
Meursault	Jehan de Massol
	Gauvain
WHITE WINES	
Aloxe-Corton	François de Salins
Meursault	Albert Grivault
	Baudot
	de Bahèzre de Lanlay
	Goureau
	Jehan Humblot
	Loppin

In a good vintage year, the Hospices de Beaune *Cuvées* may account for 500 casks, and sell for (1953) £17,600 or $53,000.

Pommard

Soon after leaving Beaune by the Route Nationale 74, a smaller country road branches off on the right and leads to the large and prosperous village of Pommard, a name second to none in point of world-wide popularity. The vineyards of Pommard were mentioned by Courtépée in A.D. 1005 and today they cover nearly a thousand acres, capable of producing, when both sun and rain have been kind, 2,640 *queues* or 264,000 gallons of fine, rather stout, red wines which require and reward long keeping. The vineyards of Pommard stretch from those of Beaune in the north to those of Volnay, in the south, without a break.

	Queues (100 gallons)
Têtes de Cuvée	
Clos Blanc	103
Les Epenots	45
Les Rugiens-Bas	33
	181 *queues*
Premières Cuvées	
Clos de la Commaraine	31
Les Petits Epenots	154
Village de Pommard	198
Other *Premières Cuvées*	838
	1,221 *queues*
Deuxièmes Cuvées	726
Troisièmes Cuvées	600
	1,326 *queues*
Grand Total	2,728 *queues*

Volnay

Volnay, immediately to the south-west of Pommard, upon higher ground, is a smaller village with only half the acreage of vineyards, but they produce a larger proportion of really high-class wines than those of Pommard. Volnay's best wines are a little lighter both in colour and body than most wines of Beaune and Pommard, but they possess great charm.

	Queues (100 gallons)
Têtes de Cuvée	
Les Angles	27
Les Caillerets	111
Les Champans	88
Les Fremiets	50
	276 *queues*
Premières Cuvées	
Clos-des-Chênes	125
Village de Volnay	103
Other *Premières Cuvées*	580
	808 *queues*
Deuxièmes Cuvées	202
Troisièmes Cuvées	358
	560 *queues*
Grand Total	1,644 *queues*

Auxey-Duresses

Auxey is one of the smaller and oldest Communes of the Côte de Beaune, and it only added the name of its best vineyard, *Duresses*, to its own, in July 1924. The village is perched upon a rocky spur on the left bank of the little Meursault river: this river separates the vineyards responsible for most red wines of the Côte de Beaune, from Savigny-les-Beaune to Monthelie, and those of a lower range of hills, from Meursault to Santenay, responsible for the finest white wines of the Côte d'Or.

Les Duresses, the only *Première Cuvée* of Auxey-Duresses, may yield up to 55 *queues*, or 5,500 gallons, of very good red wine, whilst the *Deuxièmes* and *Troisièmes Cuvées* may bring forth a total of 330 *queues* of very fair red wine. The other vineyards of this Commune yield some 440 *queues* of undistinguished wines, most of them red and some white.

Monthelie

Monthelie, further west and higher up than Auxey-Duresses, is perched upon the last tableland of the Côte de Beaune proper, overlooking the deep ravine which separates it from the Côte de Meursault. Although known by that name locally, the Côte de Meursault is more commonly included as part, the southern part, of the Côte de Beaune. Monthelie is a small village and the whole of its small territory is given up to the growing of wine-making grapes: there are no pastures, no spinneys, no ploughed fields, in fact no wasted land. The total Pinots-planted vineyards of Monthelie cannot yield, even under the most favourable climatic conditions, much more than 660 *queues* of red wine: 55 of *Premières Cuvées*, 440 of *Deuxièmes Cuvées* and 165 of *Troisièmes Cuvées*.

Meursault

Meursault is a little town with 1,500 inhabitants, its own Hôtel de Ville and Hospital, two hotels, the Chevreuil which is very good, and the Centre which is good, and a Château de Meursault, on its outskirts, the home of Comte and Comtesse de Moucheron. Meursault is the chief town of the *Côte des Blancs*, that part of the Côte d'Or which is responsible for the greatest quantity of white Burgundies and wines of greater excellence than all others. It comprises the three Communes of Meursault, Chassagne and Puligny. Although Meursault is better-known for its white wines of rare *finesse* and great charm, its vineyards produce some 660 *queues* of red wines as well as 1,100 *queues* of white wines. The vineyards of Meursault stretch from those of Volnay in the north to those of Chassagne-Montrachet in the south, without a break. All the red wines of Meursault are made from four vineyards in the north of the Commune, which adjoin those of Volnay. The best of these four vineyards, the only *Tête de Cuvée*, is called Santenots du Milieu (62 *queues*) and its wine has been known for the past 200 years as Volnay-Santenots. It is often regarded as a finer wine than any of the wines of Volnay. The other three vineyards are *Premières Cuvées*, known as Santenots de Dessus (23 *queues*), Santenots de Dessous (55 *queues*), and Les Pelures (46 *queues*): the wines of all three *climats* are entitled to the name of Volnay-Santenots. There are a further quantity of from 400 to 500 *queues* of more *ordinaires* red wines of Meursault which may be sold under their own name or as *Vins de la Côte de Beaune*.

As regards the white wines of Meursault, the finest *climat* of the Commune is Les Perrières, a *Tête de Cuvée* owned by Madame Grivault. Its optimum yield is 133 *queues* of a very délicate, fragrant and delicious white wine. Much the largest *climat* of Meursault is Les Charmes, a *Première Cuvée* with an optimum yield of

212 *queues* of a very nice white wine, all of it bv no means always identical or even comparable in quality; this is due to the fact that there are 31 different people who own a larger or smaller share of Les Charmes. Another *Première Cuvée* of Meursault, Les Genevrières, with an optimum yield of 129 *queues*, is also divided among a number of different owners, but it is a great favourite and, as such, it is "listed" by wine-merchants and hotels more frequently than any of the other Meursault *climats*, may be with the exception of Meursault Goutte d'Or. Goutte d'Or is the most popular *Deuxième Cuvée* of Meursault, with an optimum yield of 39 *queues;* this is a regrettably small quantity of wine, considering the world-wide demand for Meursault *Goutte d'Or*.

Puligny and Chassagne

These two Communes are the home, or rather the source, of the greatest of all white wines of Burgundy, *Le Montrachet*, and both added its famous name to their own in 1879, when they became Puligny-Montrachet and Chassagne-Montrachet. *Rachet*, in Burgundian parlance, means bald, and *Mont-Rachet*, which was the original spelling still to be seen on old labels, meant the "hill without a tree" [1]. The hill upon which the vines grow, which give us the famous Montrachet, is merely a mole-hill and a little more than half the vineyard is on Puligny territory, the rest on Chassagne ground.

Le Montrachet is the name of this famous vineyard and of its grand white wine; *Grand Montrachet*, is a fancy name given to the wine by some wine-merchants in their anxiety to make it clear that they are offering the one and only genuine *Montrachet*. Although under the most favourable conditions the Montrachet vineyard cannot produce more than 50 *queues* of white wine, its few acres are divided among eleven different owners: there are but three of these who own a fairly substantial slice of the Montrachet *climat*. They are the Marquis de Laguiche, the Baron Thénard, and Messrs Bouchard Père et Fils. The other eight proprietors share the remaining seven acres among them.

Besides Le Montrachet, the only *Tête de Cuvée* of both Puligny and Chassagne, there are vineyards upon all the approaches to Le Montrachet which produce excellent white wines, *Premières Cuvées* in deference to Le Montrachet, but the peers, to say the least, of the *Têtes de Cuvée* of Meursault and Aloxe-Corton. The more important of the *Premières Cuvées* of Puligny and Chassagne is *Le Bâtard-Montrachet*, more than half of it on the Chassagne side of Le Montrachet and the

---

[1]   This is why the correct pronunciation of Montrachet is *Monrachet*, without sounding the 't' of Mont, just as Montrouge is pronounced *Monrouge*.

Plate 11   BURGUNDY. Wines of the Hospices de Beaune. From the fifteenth century onwards the ancient Hospices de Beaune, still in their mediaeval glory, have been bequeathed some of the finest vine-yards of the Côte de Beaune.

Plate 12 (overleaf) THE GRAPE OF BURGUNDY AND CHAMPAGNE. The *Pinot noirien*. These blue-black grapes are covered with what looks like a light dust, but is really the natural yeast – the *Saccharomycetes* responsible for the *Mycoderma vini* or fermenting agent which will change grape-juice into wine at vintage time.

rest on the Puligny side. The optimum yield of the Bâtard-Montrachet vines is 149 *queues* of one of the really great white wines of France, a wine which has elegance and breed as well as fullness of body and power. One of the best and more reliable Bâtards-Montrachet is that which bears the name of a small but knowledgeable and honest *vigneron*, Louis Poirier by name; his home and cellars are at Pommard, where he nurses and bottles with great care the few casks of Bâtard-Montrachet that he makes every year.

	Queues (100 gallons)
Other Premières Cuvées	
Blagny Blanc	29
Champ-Canet	30
Chevalier-Montrachet	41
Les Combettes	42
Les Folatières	22
	164 *queues*
Deuxièmes Cuvées	
Les Pucelles	43
Les Referts	102
Les Sous-le-Puits	29
	174 *queues*
Grand Total	338 *queues*

Red Wines: Although the fame of both Puligny and Chassagne rests on their white wines, both Communes produce also some red wines. The optimum yield of red wines of Puligny-Montrachet is 110 *queues*, of which about one-third is *Première Cuvée* (Le Cailleret), a third *Deuxième Cuvée* (Le Clavoillon), and a third *Troisième Cuvée*. (Les Levrons and Les Charmes). Chassagne-Montrachet produces a great deal more as well as some better red wines than its twin Commune Puligny-Montrachet.

	Queues (100 gallons)
Têtes de Cuvée	
La Boudriotte	119
Le Clos Saint-Jean	95
	214 *queues*

Plate 13 (*previous page*) A BURGUNDY GRAPE. The *Gamay*. From these grapes, photographed in the *caque* or vintage basket-tray, the red wines Beaujolais are made, and all the less distinguished, also less expensive but by no means less popular, red Burgundies.

Plate 14 A BURGUNDY GRAPE. The *Aligoté*. The counterpart of the Gamay, it is used to make very pleasing white Burgundies which have not got the 'breed', nor the *bouquet*, of the aristocrats among white wines of the Côte d'Or, but are also much less expensive.

		Queues (100 *gallons*)
Premières Cuvées		
Champain		220
La Maltroie [1]		70
Other *Premières Cuvées*		146
		436 *queues*
Deuxièmes Cuvées		577
Troisièmes Cuvées		594
		1,171 *queues*
	Grand Total	1,821 *queues*

Santenay

Santenay is the last of the Communes of the Côte d'Or at its southernmost limit. Some 600 acres of Santenay vineyards are planted with noble Pinots and produce a good deal of very nice red wines, the best of them being from Les Gravières, the only *climat* of Santenay to rank as a *Tête de Cuvée;* its optimum yield is 165 *queues*.

Chalonnais, Mâconnais, Beaujolais

When it leaves Santenay, the Route Nationale 74 enters the Département of Saône-et-Loire and runs through two important towns, Chalon-sur-Saône and Mâcon, also on the Saône, to Villefranche, a distance of some sixty miles of vineyards which produce a very considerable quantity of wines, both red and white wines, but three times more reds than whites. The first section of these vineyards is called the Côte Chalonnaise. It consists of a range of hills which are the continuation of those of the Côte de Beaune, from Chagny near Santenay to Saint-Gengoux-le-National, nearly 20 miles further south, and Saint-Léger-sur-Dheune about 6 miles to the east. The hills of the Côte Chalonnaise are really the foothills of the highlands of the Charollais; they face east-south-east and the Saône Valley, with the forests of Chagny, Fontaine, Givry, Cluny and La Ferté

---

[1] There is also a very fine white wine sold under the name of Château de La Maltroie: it has been given the *Appellation Contrôlée* 'Chassagne Montrachet'.

between them and the Saône. At the northern end of the Côte Chalonnaise, the vineyards of Cheilly-les-Maranges, Dezize-les-Maranges, and Sampigny-les-Maranges actually belong, as to soil and subsoil and aspect, to the tail end of the Côte de Beaune, which is why they are entitled to the *Appellation Contrôlée* "Côte de Beaune Villages". Their best wines are the reds. A little farther south and east, that is on the way towards Chalon-sur-Saône, the wines of Chagny, Bouzeron, Rully and Montagny are either chiefly or entirely white wines, many of them quite good wines and usually good value as well, their price being appreciably below that of the Côte d'Or white wines. Then, some five miles south of Chalon-sur-Saône, Mercurey is sitting up atop a hill, completely surrounded by vineyards which stretch right and left to the Communes of Bourgneuf Val d'Or and Saint-Martin-sous-Montaign. The wines made from the vineyards of all three Communes are red wines and they are all sold under the name of *Mercurey*. They are the best red wines of the Côte Chalonnaise, challenged only for quality by the red wines of Givry, at the southernmost limit of the Côte Chalonnaise, and a short distance only from Mercurey.

We then come to the Côte Mâconnaise which has much more *méridional* character, quite different from the Burgundian. It begins at or near Tournus, a quaint old mediaeval town on the river Saône, with flat-roofed houses as in Provence and Italy, where they have no fear of snow. The Côte Mâconnaise proper ends at Romanèche, where the Saône-et-Loire ends and where the Beaujolais begins, but the vineyards of both Mâconnais and Beaujolais are really one, an immense stretch of vines covering hundreds and hundreds of acres, as far as the eye can see, from the river Saône, in the east, to great tree-capped mountains in the west. The vineyards of the Mâconnais and Beaujolais produce more wine than all the other vineyards of Burgundy put together; their wines are mostly red and made from Gamay grapes. Until the latter part of the last century, these wines were commonly known as *Vins de Mâcon*, but now the name of Beaujolais has acquired a measure of public favour so great as to be embarrassing: the demand for Beaujolais in Paris alone is reckoned to be about twice as great as the supply of genuine Beaujolais.

The popularity of Beaujolais is due to a certain extent to the appeal of its pretty name, but chiefly to the fact that of all *ordinaires* red table wines it is the most acceptable within eighteen months, or even twelve, of its vintage, or birth: it has a soft, fruity quality that is very attractive and its cost is or should be much less than that of red wines which have to be kept for five or more years before they are fit to drink.

Not only much but most of the red wines of the Mâconnais and Beaujolais are sold as *Beaujolais* or *Mâcon rouge*, but there are others, many other and better wines both red and white which are sold under the names of the vineyards of their birth. Of the reds, the best are the wines of Moulin-à-Vent, a name which covers a multitude of red wines made from the vineyards of Romanèche-Thorins, just in the Mâconnais, and those of the adjoining Commune of Chenas, just in the Beaujolais. Again, as a Moulin-à-Vent wine is a better and dearer wine, usually also an older one than a plain Beaujolais, there are a number of Moulin-à-Vent vineyards responsible for better wines than the rest and these are sold with the name of their vineyard, such as *Clos de Rochegrès*, *Clos des Jacques*, *Clos du Carquelin*, etc. The Moulin-à-Vent *Château de Chenas* is the name given to the wines of the Cave Co-opérative of Chenas.

Among the other particularly good and justly popular red wines sold under the name of their native village, mention should be made of Brouilly and Côte de Brouilly, Chiroubles, Fleurie, Juliénas, Morgon, Romanèche-Thorins and Saint-Amour.

At Romanèche-Thorins, the Hospices, like the Hospices de Beaune but on a smaller scale, bottle at the Hospices their wines which are sold as *Moulin-à-Vent des Hospices de Romanèche-Thorins*, a blend always of dependable quality of Moulin-à-Vent wines.

As regards the white wines of the Mâconnais-Beaujolais, there are none better than those of Pouilly, Chaintré, Vergisson, Fuissé, Vinzelles and Loché, all of them on or near the great rock of Solutré, a short distance to the north-west of Romanèche-Thorins. Pouilly is not a Commune but a mere hamlet of the Commune of Solutré. Its white wine, however, is considered the best of the bunch, and its neighbours have tacked on its name to their own, Pouilly-Fuissé being used for the wines not only of Pouilly and Fuissé but also for those of Solutré, Vergisson and Chaintré, whereas the wines of Vinzelles and Loché are made by the *Cave Co-Opérative* of each village and are sold as Pouilly-Vinzelles and Pouilly-Loché.

The white wines of Pouilly-Fuissé have become so popular that the demand has outgrown the supply. There are, of course, perfectly genuine Pouilly-Fuissé wines sold under that name and no other, but one can be quite sure not only of a genuine Pouilly-Fuissé wine but of one of the better ones if the label on the bottle also bears the name of a particular vineyard or Estate, such as Château de Fuissé, at Fuissé; Le Clos, at Pouilly; Le Mont Garcin, at Solutré; Les Charmes, at Vergisson; or Le Paradis, at Chaintré.

La Confrérie des Chevaliers du Tastevin

The economic crisis of the early nineteen thirties was world-wide. It may or it may not have been an inevitable consequence of the post-war boom but it was certainly aggravated in Burgundy by the failure of three successive vintages, 1930, 1931 and 1932. The big firms, the "Shippers", with great cellars full of 1928, 1929 and older excellent wines, for which the demand was not nearly as keen as it would have been under more normal, let alone prosperous circumstances, could well afford to wait for the return of good vintages. But the thousands of small vineyard owners, the great majority of the Burgundy *vignerons*, who had far too slender financial reserves to face a three years' failure, were in desperate straits. It was then that some of the more public-minded business men of Nuits-Saint-Georges decided to form an association of *vignerons* and merchants to devise the best means of attracting more visitors to Burgundy and of increasing the demand for the wines of Burgundy. This is how, in January 1933, was formed the *Syndicat d'Initiative de Nuits-Saint-Georges*, the egg laid by Georges Faiveley and Camille Rodier, out of which was hatched, in 1934, the *Confrérie des Chevaliers du Tastevin*.

In Burgundy, as in Champagne, the beginning of October is usually vintage time and the new wine generally "falls bright", that is it has got over its first fermenting fever by the end of November: it can then be tasted and tested for the first time. This is why there was for a great many years a *Journée des Vins de Nuits* and a *Paulée de Meursault* during the last week in November, when *vignerons* and merchants met at Nuits-Saint-Georges, to taste the red wines of the Côte de Nuits, and at Meursault, to taste the white wines of the Côte de Beaune, and not merely to taste wines but to talk about them as well as to eat and drink and make merry. It was also on the last Sunday in November that the new wines of the *Hospices de Beaune* were offered for sale by public auction. It is to the undying credit of the *Confrérie des Chevaliers du Tastevin* to have made of those three days a wonderful triptych with the *Hospices de Beaune* Sunday auction in the centre panel, the *Confrérie's* Saturday Banquet on the left and the Monday *Paulée de Meursault* on the right, three festive days now known all the world over as *Les Trois Glorieuses*, three days devoted to the glory of the wines of Burgundy.

The banquet staged on the eve of the *Hospices* public auction by the *Confrérie des Chevaliers du Tastevin* is the culminating function of the Annual *Chapitre*, when new *Chevaliers* are "knighted" with great pomp and ceremony, choruses and trumpeting, scarlet robes and ermine facings, a most spectacular not to say theatrical setting which attracts crowds of people not only to the Château du Clos Vougeot, now the headquarters of the *Confrérie*, but to the *Hospices de Beaune* auction the next day, and to Meursault, the day after. And all these people,

Chevaliers du Tastevin or not, know much more about Burgundy than they ever did before; they and their friends also know and like the wines of Burgundy better than they ever did before. So much so, that the Burgundy *vignerons* have now no difficulty in selling all the wine they make year by year.

The success achieved by the *Confrérie des Chevaliers du Tastevin* was so rapid and so complete that the wine-growers and wine-merchants of other districts were not slow in following so good an example and it was not very long before there was a *Jurade de Saint-Emilion*, a *Commanderie du Bontemps du Médoc*, a *Confrérie des Sacavins d'Anjou*, *Chevaliers du Cep*, and others. [1]

[1] LES CONFRERIES VINEUSES DE FRANCE

ALSACE. Confrérie de Saint Etienne

ARMAGNAC. Compagnie des Mousquetaires d'Armagnac

BERGERAC. Consulat de la Vinée de Bergerac

BORDEAUX. Jurade de Saint Emilion
Commanderie du Bontemps du Médoc
Connétablie de Guyenne

BOURGOGNE. Confrérie des Chevaliers du Tastevin
Compagnons du Beaujolais
Confrérie des Vignerons de Saint-Vincent de Mâcon

COGNAC. Principauté de Franc-Pineau

COTES DE PROVENCE. Ordre illustre des Chevaliers de la Méduse

GAILLAC. Confrérie de la Dive Bouteille

JURA. Compagnons du Bouju

JURANÇON. Viguerie royale de Jurançon

LANGUEDOC. Les Maistres Tastaïres du Languedoc

SAVOIE. Confrérie du Sarto-Savoyard

VAL DE LOIRE et CENTRE. Confrérie des Sacavins d'Anjou
Confrérie des Chevaliers de la Chantepleure
Ordre des Chevaliers-de Bretvins
Les Baillis de Pouilly-sur-Loire
Confrérie des Tire-Douzil
Confrérie des Vignerons de Saint-Vincent de Tannay

TOUTES REGIONS : Ordre universel et militant des Chevaliers du Cep.

CHAPTER FOUR

Champagne

CHAMPAGNE IS, TODAY, the festive wine *par excellence*, the most lively and one of the most expensive of quality wines, a joy and a luxury. But it was not ever thus. During many centuries the wines of the great Champagne Province, stretching from Flanders in the north to Burgundy in the south, and from Lorraine in the east to the Ile de France in the west, were plain, still, table wines, mostly red. Whether better or not than the wines of Bordeaux and Burgundy is anybody's guess, but they can certainly claim, without fear of contradiction, to have been French much longer. It was only in the 15th century that the English lost Bordeaux and its wines, and it was only in the 16th century that the Emperor Charles V finally surrendered Burgundy to France. But it was in A.D. 496 that Saint Remi, Bishop of Reims, received into the Church Clovis, first Christian King of the Franks, and all Kings of France have been crowned at Reims ever since.

That there was wine in Champagne in those early days is no mere speculation; there is ample documentary evidence of it, since we still possess Saint Remi's own *Testament* in which there are several Champagne vineyards mentioned among his legacies. Nor can there be any doubt about the excellence of the wines of Champagne of long ago since they were praised by Pope Urbain II (1088–1099) and 500 years later by Pope Leo X (1513–1521). The wines of Champagne had no other competitors in Paris than those of Orléans and Touraine, until the 17th century when both Bordeaux and Burgundy also sent in their wines. The wines of Burgundy were the more dangerous competitors of the two; they were of the same grape, the Pinot, and of the same type as the wines of Champagne, and they were very likely better wines, to judge from the still table wines of Champagne made today compared to the still table wines of Burgundy of the same vintages.

There is, therefore, every reason to assume that the *vignerons* of Champagne sought to produce a wine that would be, if not better, at least different from any wine that had ever come out of Burgundy, and eventually Sparkling Champagne proved to be the right answer. This is where Dom Pérignon comes in.

Dom Pérignon was born at Sainte-Menehoulde in January, 1639. He renounced the world at the early age of nineteen and never regretted it. In 1668, when only in his thirtieth year, he was appointed to the post of Cellarer of the Benedictine Abbey of Hautvillers, near Epernay, in the Champagne country.

Plate 15 CHAMPAGNE. The vintage at Mareuil-sur-Ay. The picked *Pinot noir* grapes have been gathered and assembled under the eye of the *Maître de vendange*, each *caque* contains many kilos of grapes and the ticket records the vineyards and the name of the *vendangeur*. From thence the grapes will be taken to the *pressoir* to be crushed, where their sweet juice will be collected in vats away from the blue-black skins with a crimson lining, which is not allowed to contact and colour the juice.

During forty-seven consecutive years, until the day of his death, in September, 1715, Dom Pérignon was in charge of the cellars and of the finances of the Abbey. He had a remarkably keen palate and knew how to use it to good purpose. He had great experience in all matters pertaining to viticulture and wine-making; he was hardworking and shrewd; he made better wines than had ever been made before at Hautvillers; he also made some sparkling wine. He was a good man, he loved the poor.

So much, and very little more, is tolerably certain.

Dom Pérignon has been hailed as the discoverer, inventor or creator of sparkling Champagne. He has been described as the wizard who first put the bubbles into Champagne.

This is mere romance. Dom Pérignon did not discover, invent or create sparkling Champagne. He never claimed to have done so, nor did any of his contemporaries claim any such honour for him. He would certainly have greatly resented being hailed as the first to have "put bubbles into Champagne", when neither he nor anybody else ever put bubbles into Champagne. The bubbles of sparkling Champagne are the same as the bubbles of bottled beer: they are tiny drops of liquid disturbed, chased and whipped by escaping carbon dioxide or carbonic acid gas. This carbon dioxide is an inevitable by-product of a most natural phenomenon known as fermentation.

Champagne is a cold-blooded northerner. It begins fermenting cheerfully enough but thinks better of it and settles down to a long sleep during the winter months. In the following spring or early summer, it wakes up and takes up its half-finished job where it had left it. There is still some of the original grape-juice sugar left to be fermented, and after their long winter rest, the saccharomy-cetes will now get busy again and supply the necessary zymase. In fact, to make sure that they will have plenty to do, a little more sugar is added to the wine which is then bottled and corked securely down.

Exactly the same thing goes on within the bottle as in the cask, but with this difference, that the carbonic acid gas can no longer lose itself in the air; it re-mains in solution in the wine, a most amenable prisoner so long as there is no hope of escape. But once that gate of its prison, the cork, has gone, it rushes out of the wine with joy, carrying along in its haste thousands of dewdrops of wine; these are the Champagne "bubbles".

Dom Pérignon did not create sparkling Champagne, but he did a great deal for its fame. He made better wines than had been made in Champagne before, both still and sparkling. The excellence of Dom Pérignon's wines was due to the art with which he blended the grapes from various vineyards. It was due also to the fact that the Abbey of Hautvillers owned more vineyards and received by way of tithes a greater variety of grapes than any private vineyard owner.

Plate 16 A CHAMPAGNE GRAPE. The *Pinot Vert Doré*. Champagne may be made from either or both the two Pinot grapes: *Noir* or *Blanc*. When made from the Pinot blanc alone, it may be called Blanc de blancs. The main Pinot blanc vineyards are those of the left bank of the Marne, near Epernay, along the road from Pierry to Vertus, pas-sing through Cramant, Avize, Le Mesnil and Oger. This grape is also used for the making of the finest white Burgundies.

Situated as they are so close to the northern latitude beyond which grapes will grow but will hardly ever fully ripen, the vineyards of Champagne are not blessed, nor were they blessed in the seventeenth century, with their full quota of sunshine year after year. They only enjoy a really fine summer now and again and they produce then, but only then, grapes which give wonderful wine, wine truly deserving to be enjoyed and remembered as a vintage wine. Such years are the exception; other years, poorer years, years of acid, sun-starved wine, are the rule.

Just as reservoirs and irrigation have banished the spectre of famine in many sub-tropical countries, so judicious blending has brought fame and riches to the old province of Champagne. By saving wines of the better years and by finding out which blends of various vineyards will harmonize and give the best results, a very much higher level of average excellence has been reached and stocks of wines of fairly uniform quality have been built which have enabled the Champagne shippers to dispense for years and years to a suffering humanity that most exhilarating form of relaxation known throughout the civilized world as sparkling Champagne.

Dom Pérignon was the first to show the way; he was not the first to make sparkling wine nor to use corks, but he was the first to show the people of Champagne what was the best use they could make of their wines. It is not only the wine-growers and wine-shippers of Champagne who owe Dom Pérignon a deep debt of gratitude, but all who appreciate the charm of sparkling Champagne, all those to whom Champagne has brought at some time or other that which is worth more than gold and silver: health and joy.

If there is one man who deserves to share with Dom Pérignon the gratitude of all true Champagne lovers, it is François, the man who first showed how sparkling Champagne could be made with any degree of scientific precision and by so doing placed the whole of the Champagne trade upon a sound commercial basis. He did this by inventing the *densimètre*, the all-important instrument which measures with precision the amount of sugar in the *must* at the time of bottling. Before the *densimètre*, it was left to the uncertain taste of man; too much sugar, the bottles burst; too little sugar, flat wine. The *densimètre* removed the element of uncertainty.

From the days of Dom Pérignon to those of François, that is roughly 150 years, from 1690 to 1840, the vogue of sparkling Champagne had many ups and downs – mostly downs. There were all through that period a large class of connoisseurs who made no secret of their dislike of the "green" sparkling wines of Epernay, and who definitely preferred the still wines of the Montagne de Reims. Still Champagne had a far greater number of admirers, in France, than the sparkling variety, which seems to have been synonymous with "new" Champagne. In England, the Dry Sillery and other still or barely creaming wines of

Reims also had many supporters. Thus, in a letter written, in 1788, to Mr Moët, at Epernay, by Messrs Carbonnell, Moody & Walker, London wine-merchants, they asked for twenty dozen of Champagne to be shipped to them in two hampers of ten dozen each, adding that "the wine must be of good quality, not too charged with liqueur, but of excellent taste and not at all sparkling".

Before François, there was no scientific means of ascertaining the quantity of unfermented sugar in the wine and the most costly mistakes were made. According to Jullien, the proportion of bottles which burst in Champagne cellars and were consequently a total loss, varied from 15 per cent to 40 per cent in 1816. In 1833, the loss in Mr Moët's cellars, at Epernay, was 35 per cent and, in 1834, 25 per cent. In 1842, according to the Académie de Reims, the loss due to "*casse en caves*" was only 10 per cent. Since François, others, and more particularly Maumené in 1858, Robinet in 1877, and Salleron in 1889, have brought the science of making sparkling wines to such perfection that the number of burst bottles in Champagne cellars is now very small indeed.

When François's methods were generally adopted, the Champagne trade became much more profitable and less hazardous. Many new firms then came into existence and, in order to make their wines known to the public, offered them at low prices which had hitherto never been thought to be within the range of possibilities.

Thus it came to pass that the average sales of Champagne rose from some thirteen million bottles per annum during the 'sixties, to nineteen million during the 'seventies and over twenty-two million during the 'eighties and 'nineties.

The sales of Champagne increased rapidly, but not nearly in the same proportion in all markets. In France, for instance, the sale of Champagne remained practically stationary from 1861 – when a total of 6,904, 914 bottles of Champagne were exported to all parts of the world – to 1890 – when the total exports of Champagne had risen to 21,699,108 bottles. During the same time, the consumption of Champagne in England rose from about three to over nine million bottles per annum, as the result of the introduction of dry Champagne in England, whilst the sweet "dessert" type of Champagne remained the rule throughout France.

The Making of Sparkling Champagne

It is now time to consider in what way the making of sparkling champagne differs from the methods for making a natural wine described in Chapter VI on 'The Art of Wine making'.

Sparkling Champagne is a white wine made mostly from Pinot grapes that we call black, but they are not black; their juice is white and their skin is blue outside and red inside. To make a white wine from black grapes is not done by magic, but by care and skill. The colouring pigment of so-called black grapes is contained in the lining of their skin so that grapes must be picked and brought to the press unbruised and without delay if their white juice is not to be dyed pink before they are pressed. In Champagne, the grapes are picked with care as soon as they are ripe, but before being sent to the *pressoir* to be crushed they are first examined at the roadside nearest the vineyard of their birth by a team of women, mostly elderly ones who have had their full share of back-breaking grape-picking when they were younger: they sit in a row with a wide osier tray at knee height before them; the grapes gathered by the pickers are brought to the women at the roadside in baskets which are tipped over onto the osier tray. The women quickly take up and look over bunch after bunch, removing expertly with a pair of long pointed scissors all defective berries, if and when there happens to be any, either unripe or mildewy, or otherwise undesirable for any cause whatsoever. All such "rejects" are dropped in a refuse bin whilst the bunches with none but sound and ripe grapes go into great osier baskets known as *caques*. These are then loaded on lorries and driven to the nearest *vendangeoir* of the person or firm who owns the vineyard or who has bought the grapes from the *vignerons*. At the *vendangeoir*, the grapes are weighed in their *caques* and tipped out into the *pressoir* until there is enough for a pressing or "charge", usually of 4,000 kilogs. or nearly 4 tons. The bunches are kept whole, not *égrappées* nor *foulées* as in Burgundy or the Gironde, and the grapes remain whole when tipped in the *pressoir*. This consists of a square wooden floor with four adjustable open-work wooden rails which make a sort of cage in which the grapes are heaped. The *pressoir* has a heavy lid of oak boards which is lowered and raised at will by a screw now driven, as a rule, by electricity but until recently by muscle and sweat. When the lid is clamped on the heaped grapes in the *pressoir*, and slowly but relentlessly driven down, its crushing pressure bursts the grapes and their sweet juice immediately runs off through the rails into a slightly sloping wide groove that leads it to a collecting "station" without having been in contact for any time with the skins of the grapes; these are left behind in the cage of the press. The first flow pressed out of the grapes is either led or pumped into a vat which holds 450 gallons of this the best grape juice or *Cuvée*. Greater pressure is then applied and more juice is squeezed out of the wet husks still in the cage of the *pressoir*, but it is neither as white nor as sweet nor as good as the *Cuvée*, and it is not mixed with it. Very soon after the *Cuvée* has been vatted, it begins to ferment in a rather boisterous manner, throwing off an ugly "head" or scum, thus getting rid of any dirt or dust or anything else which is not wanted; some of which, the heavier stuff, falls at the bottom of the vat as lees. When the "*must*", as this working grape-juice is called, returns to a more normal temperature, in 24 or 36 hours, as a rule, all that is clear is drawn into 10 clean oak casks holding 44 gallons each, and these casks are sent at once by lorry to Reims, Epernay, Ay, or wherever the persons or firms who own the wine-to-be have their cellars. All through the vintage, which may be long or short according to the more or less favourable weather conditions from year to year, lorries are busy day and night fetching casks to put the new wine in and delivering full ones at the *celliers* from all parts of the Champagnes vineyards. During the next eight to ten weeks, the "*must*" will be left alone and will gradually become new wine, most of the grape-sugar present in the "*must*" having become alcohol which stays put, and carbonic acid gas, which loses itself in the air.

The new wines are then racked, that is transferred into new casks, leaving behind the sediment cast off during the process of fermentation. After being racked, the new wines of different pressings or *marcs* of each vineyard or set of vineyards are "assembled" or blended together, in order to obtain one standard wine from each place, irrespective of whether the wine was made at the beginning of the vintage or at the end, from grapes which might have been hardly fully ripe in the first instance and from may be slightly overripe grapes in the second. The newly racked and "assembled" wine is given another four or five weeks to rest and to proceed a little further with its slow fermentation, if it has a mind to do so. It is then racked another time, which serves the double purpose of separating it from any lees it may have cast off, and to give it plenty of fresh air. Then comes the all-important business of making-up the *Cuvées*. The *Chef de Caves*, whose responsibility it is, must taste with the greatest keenness the wines of all the different vineyards or sets of vineyards, and he has to decide how much or how little of the wines of each different district he ought to blend together to secure the approximate right quantity and quality of each one of the different brands which his firm sells on different markets, in competition with other Champagne Shippers. The *Chef de Caves* may also decide to add to his *Cuvées* more or less of older wines which have been kept in cask for that very purpose. When, after many tastings and much hesitation, his choice has been made, the chosen wines are mixed and blended together in great *foudres* or vats with an electrically actioned mechanical arm churning the wines thoroughly; after which they are tested for sugar, liqueured and bottled.

The style of each *Cuvée* depends entirely upon the skill and taste of the *Chef de Caves*, but the quality of the wine depends in the first place upon the quality of the grapes which, in Champagne as everywhere else, varies with the soil, sub-soil and aspect of different vineyards. No *Chef de Caves*, however skilled he may be in the art of blending, can possibly make a first-quality wine out of second-quality grapes. A Champagne *Cuvée* made from different wines from none but the very best vineyards would not be an economic or commercial proposition, but the best *Cuvées* are always those in which there is a greater proportion of *Premiers Crus* grapes, a smaller proportion of *Deuxièmes Crus* and no *Troisièmes Crus* at all.

The quantity of *"liqueur de tirage"* which is added at bottling time to the *Cuvée de tirage* is such that the newly bottled wine will have just the right proportion of carbonic acid gas to make it as sparkling as it should be, no less and no more, after fermentation will have intervened. This *liqueur de tirage* is plain sugar candy melted in Champagne wine. When the *Cuvée de tirage* is bottled, its cork is held by a strong clamp which will keep it safely in the bottle at the *"prise de mousse"*, that is, when fermentation does its job. As soon as bottled, the *Cuvée de tirage* is laid to rest in the deep, damp, cold, chalk cellars of Reims, Epernay and Ay, to be left alone for two or three years: long before that, the wine will have fermented out any of the sugar that was in it when it was bottled. It will be sparkling Champagne right enough, but not fit to drink. During its bottle fermentation, the wine throws off small but none the less objectionable pieces of tartaric acid, mucilage and other matters of either mineral or vegetable origin. This sediment lies quietly enough in the safely corked bottle, but it would foul the look and taste of the wine the moment glasses were filled. So it must be taken out of the wine somehow and this is done most skilfully by the *remuage* and *dégorgement*. The *remuage* consists in giving each bottle, day after day, a twist sharp enough to make the sediment slide down towards the neck of the bottle, but not hard enough to make it rise into the wine. The process begins with the bottle in a horizontal position but when completed the bottle stands vertically, neck downwards, and by that time the whole of the sediment has been gathered upon the inside face of the cork.

The next move is the removing of the cork with its wad of sediment, so that the wine be absolutely "star bright" and will remain like it to the last drop. This must be done, and it is done with practically no loss of wine and very little loss of the precious gas in it. The man who does it, *le dégorgeur*, is a skilled and valuable man indeed. He is the first of a team who deal with the bottle of sparkling Champagne when the time has come to make it ready to leave the depths of the Cellars and go into the world. Next to the *dégorgeur* comes the *doseur*, the man who adds to the bottle of wine more or less *Liqueur d'Expédition*, a very sticky mixture of sugar, still Champagne wine and brandy: the wine to melt the sugar, the sugar to sweeten the wine, and the brandy to stop the sugar fermenting. The object of this addition of *Liqueur d'Expédition* is to give to the wine just the degree of sweetness which is to the taste of the customer: it may be as little as ½% if the wine is for people who like *Brut Champagne*, 1% for those who prefer *Extra Sec*, 3% for those who prefer *Sec* and 5% for the *Demi-Sec* connoisseurs. All such proportions are only approximate since each Champagne Shipper has his own technique in preparing the *Liqueur d'Expédition* and using it. When the *doseur* has done his job, he passes on the bottle to the *boucheur* who drives into the neck of the bottle a long and fat branded cork, which has to be forcibly squeezed to half its natural size for half its length to fit in the neck of the bottle. Next to the *boucheur* sits the *ficeleur*, who squashes down the half of the cork jutting out of the neck and makes it fast to the ring of the bottle neck with a 3-branch or 4-branch wire. The bottle of Sparkling Champagne is then ready; when the call comes, it is sent up from the Cellars to the Cellier where it is washed, dressed up, packed up and sent off.

Champagne bottles are the most gaily decorated of all wines: body labels and shoulder *collerettes* are not peculiar to Champagne but the bright or dull "foil", the sheet of gold, silver or coloured metal or paper which covers the cork and the whole of the neck of the bottle makes it look festive, but its purpose in the beginning was purely utilitarian. Instead of the wire which now holds down the final cork, the *bouchon d'expédition*, string was originally used and it was protected from damp and rats by a tightly fitting pewter cap with a dab of one colour or another over it to differentiate different wines. Gradually this protective pewter, growing more and more ornate and longer, became the Champagne foil as we know it today.

Vintage and Non-Vintage Champagne

A Vintage Champagne is, or ought to be, the wine made from Pinot grapes grown in Champagne vineyards in one and the same year, the date of which it bears, printed on its labels and branded upon its corks. The vineyards of Champagne are very near the northern limit beyond which grapes will not mature in the open, and Champagne grapes do not ripen fully unless there has been a particularly hot summer. There are, unfortunately, a number of years when the weather is not all that it should be, and the wines made in such years are likely to be somewhat tart and thin. Then it is that those wealthy Champagne Shippers with immense reserves of wines of past good vintages bring forth the right quantity of soft and fat wine to blend with the others, and they often do produce in this manner very nice wines indeed which cannot be sold under the date of any one particular year, but they are none the less quite good wines, often better value than Vintage wines.

Vintage wines possess, naturally, a greater degree of personality and they age more graciously, especially when they are really self-wines – not assisted or "bettered" by the addition of older wines. They also invariably cost more than non-vintage Champagne; in the first place because they are, or ought to be, better wines, and in the second because there is a limited quantity of any Vintage Cuvée; sooner or later the time must come when there will be no more; when that time approaches, the scarcer and dearer the wines become.

The Champagne District

The old Champagne Province was divided in 1790 into four Départements, Aisne and Haute-Marne in the north, Marne in the centre, and Aube in the south. There are vineyards in all four Départements but the fact that the roots of their vines are in Champagne soil is not sufficient to give to the wine made from their grapes the right to the name of Champagne. The soil, sub-soil and aspect of the vineyards must be such that the noble Pinots can thrive and produce a wine worthy to bear the honoured name of Champagne. This is why the limits of the *région délimitée*, the only area allowed to call its wines Champagne, have been drawn and fixed by law. This official *région délimitée* covers a total of, roughly speaking, 27,000 acres, of which 21,000 are in the Marne Département, 4,600 in the Aube, and 1,400 in the Aisne. Obviously, although these 27,000 acres of vineyards are legally entitled to call their wines Champagne, there are very great differences in the quality of their wines. We can, without any hesitation, discard, to begin with, the wines of the Aube and Aisne vineyards. They produce none but the cheaper qualities of Champagne which are drunk either locally or in Paris night-clubs. All the better-quality Champagne comes from the vineyards of the Marne Département, which does not mean, unfortunately, that all the vineyards of the Marne Département produce automatically very high quality wines.

There are in the Marne, as in the Côte d'Or and the Gironde, vineyards which are either very much better or just a little better than others. It depends chiefly upon the nature of soil and sub-soil, and also on the altitude and aspect of each vineyard. The climate is the same for all, although some may be more sheltered than others. In Champagne the weather is often bitter in winter, but the vines do not mind hard frost when dormant; spring is the most dangerous time of the year, as late frosts may do and often do incalculable damage.

Summers are often very hot, with occasional thunderstorms and hailstorms; autumn, vintage time, is often warm and sunny, which makes everybody very happy; a wet and cold vintage spells disaster. It was ever thus, or, at any rate, for the past 1000 years; we can be fairly certain of the age-long uncertainty of the weather in Champagne because records still exist of the prices paid at the vintage time from the tenth century to our own day, and they show that prices soared when spring frosts had brought about a shortage of wine, but slumped badly when there was a glut. In 1952, when a moderate quantity (7,354,000 gallons) of very fine wine was made, the best grapes were sold at 155 francs per kilog., roughly equivalent to $ 5.60 or 40s. per gallon of wine. In 1953, when rather less (7,000,000 gallons) of a fair quality wine was made, the price rose to 160 francs per kilog. for the best grapes, or about $ 5.88 or 42s. per gallon of wine. In 1954, there was a greater quantity (8,344,000 gallons) of wine made, but of very poor quality, in spite of which the best grapes had to be paid for at the rate of 138 francs per kilog., or about $ 4.76 or 34s. per gallon of wine. Happily, 1955 was a better year in every respect, and there were 10,351,000 gallons of wine made and the quality of most of it was very good indeed; the best grapes were paid for at the rate of 141 francs per kilog., which is roughly equivalent to $ 5.04 or 36s. per gallon, that is 84 cents or 6s. per bottle of raw material, the rough wine which will require a hundred pairs of hands and at least six years to become the brilliant sparkling wine in a gaily dressed bottle that will be offered to us for sale – and at what price?

All the better vineyards of the Marne have been divided into many classes or categories according to the quality of the wine which may be expected from their grapes: the best are in what is called the *Catégorie Grand Cru* and the next three in *Première*, *Deuxième* and *Troisième Catégorie*. When vintage time is at hand, the Champagne shippers and the growers, whose grapes the shippers are going to buy, meet and agree upon what shall be the right price to pay for the grapes of the *Catégorie Grand Cru* vineyards, and that settles the price of the grapes of the remaining categories; they are paid for according to an agreed descending scale, from 100% to 90% of the maximum price for *Première Cru* wines (the wines of this category rated at 100% are the *Grand Crus*); wines below 90% are of lesser quality. The margin allows for paying more or less according to quality, since all the wines of the same *Catégorie* are not likely to be identical. Some *vignerons* may have taken greater care or they may have had better luck than others.

Here is, in alphabetical order for easier reference, a list of the better growths of the Marne Département:–

Catégorie Hors-Classe	*Deuxième Catégorie*	*Troisième Catégorie*
Ambonnay	Avenay	Chamery
Avize	Bergères-les-Vertus	Coulommes-la-Montagne
Ay-Champagne	Bisseuil	Damery
Beaumont-sur-Vesle	Champillon	Ecueil
Bouzy	Chigny-les-Roses	Epernay
Cramant	Chouilly	Jouy
Louvois	Cuis	Mancy
Mailly	Cumières	Monthelon
Sillery	Grauves	Moussy
Verzenay	Hautvillers	Pargny
	Ludes	Puisieulx
Première Catégorie	Mutigny	Sacy
Dizy	Pierry	Saint-Thierry
Le Mesnil-sur-Oger	Rilly-la-Montagne	Sermiers
Mareuil-sur-Ay	Trépail	Venteuil
Oger	Vaudemanges	Vinay
Oiry	Vertus	Vrigny
Tauxières	Villedommange	
Tours-sur-Marne	Villers-Allerand	
Verzy	Villers-Marmery	

Nearly all these vineyards are in the *Arrondissements* of Reims and Epernay, and a few only in the Canton of Vertus, of the *Arrondissement* of Châlons-sur-Marne. They cover the approaches to the Montagne de Reims and its lower slopes facing Reims and Châlons-sur-Marne; the hillsides upon the right bank of the river Marne above and below Epernay; and the approaches and lower slopes of a range of gentle hills some distance to the left of the Marne, above Epernay, known as the Montagne d'Avize or Côte des Blancs.

Montagne de Reims

The Montagne de Reims is a cliff of tertiary formation and in the shape of a flat iron with its sharp end pointing eastwards towards Châlons-sur-Marne; it rises sharply from the billowing plain crossed by the little river Vesle, on the north-east, and from the banks of the Marne, on the south-west. A great forest and wild boar sanctuary covers the broad crest of the Montagne de Reims, but its sides and approaches are covered with closely planted vineyards on all sides. That part of the Montagne de Reims on the Vesle side, and farthest away from Châlons-sur-Marne, is known as *La Petite Montagne*, and its vineyards produce the less distinguished wines entitled to the name of Champagne; the best of them, however, those of Sacy and Villedommange, are in good demand, being cheaper than most and considered to be very good value. Leaving *La Petite Montagne* for *La Montagne* and proceeding eastwards, we shall pass through the vineyards of Villers-Allerand, Rilly-la-Montagne, Chigny-les-Roses, Ludes, Mailly-Champagne, Verzenay, Verzy and Villers-Marmery, all of them hillside villages and vineyards, whilst we shall survey from our vantage point – none of greater beauty than the Moulin de Verzenay – a wonderful panorama of flourishing vineyards, including those of Sillery and Beaumont-sur-Vesle stretching to the Route Nationale from Reims to Châlons-sur-Marne.

All these "Montagne" vineyards are practically back-to-back with the "Marne" vineyards on the other side, but there are others at the eastern end, or turning point of the Montagne, forming a sort of connecting link between the two: they are the vineyards of Trépail, Tauxières and Louvois, on the Châlons-sur-Marne side, and Bouzy and Ambonnay on the Marne side. We shall then turn our backs on Châlons-sur-Saône, and, facing Château-Thierry and Paris farther west, we shall pass through the riverside vineyards of Bisseuil, Mareuil-sur-Ay, Avenay and Ay, a little town as quaint as its name and well worth a visit. Beyond Ay, the vineyards of Dizy-Magenta and Cumières, and those of Champillon and Hautvillers much higher up, all produce very fine wines but the same cannot fairly be said of the wines made from grapes grown farther west upon the right bank of the Marne, practically as far as Château-Thierry.

Some 80% of the grapes grown in all these vineyards are black Pinot grapes, with patches of white Pinot-Chardonnay grapes here and there, chiefly at Verzy. There are, in Champagne as in Burgundy, different kinds of Pinots noirs, the best, or at any rate the one which is grown to a greater extent than all others, is that which is known locally by the name of *plant doré*, of which there are three slightly different sorts, known as *Le Petit Plant doré*, *Le Gros Plant doré d'Ay* and *Le Vert doré* which is also sometimes known as *Plant Jeanson* or *Plant d'Ay*.

Other varieties are the *Plant Gris*, which has nothing to do with the *Pinot gris*, a white grape; it is also known as *Pinot de Trépail* and *Pinot de Vertus*. All these are "noble" Pinots, but they have a poor relation, the *Pinot Meunier*, with more and heavier bunches of grapes but giving a commoner type of wine.

On the left bank of the Marne, the better wines are those of Chouilly and Pierry, close to Epernay, to the right and left of the town, but the best wines are those of a range of gentle hills a little farther back from the river; they rise soon after one leaves Pierry and stretch as far as Vertus. This is the part of the *Champagne viticole* known as *La Côte des Blancs*, or the hill of the white grapes, where the white Pinot-Chardonnay grapes are grown almost exclusively. It is also called *Blanc de Cramant*, or *Pinot blanc Chardonnay*. The most important township of the Côte des Blancs is Avize, with Cramant on higher ground to its right, or west, Le Mesnil, Oger and Vertus to its left, or east. The other vineyards of the Côte des Blancs, those of Monthelon and Cuis, on the Pierry side of Cramant, and Grauves on the other side of the same hill, also produce white wine from white grapes, "Blanc de Blancs", entitled to the name of Champagne, but they are of distinctly plainer quality.

The immense stretches of vines, so closely planted, which meet the eye of the visitor, give no idea of how small are most of the holdings of individual owners of the Champagne vineyards, but according to official statistics the vineyards of the Marne are divided among 11,298 proprietors, in the following proportions:–

4,300	own less than $\frac{1}{2}$ acre each
4,770	own more than $\frac{1}{2}$ acre and less than $2\frac{1}{2}$ acres
2,080	own more than $2\frac{1}{2}$ acres and less than 12 acres
87	own more than 12 acres and less than 25 acres
38	own more than 25 acres and less than 50 acres
18	own more than 50 acres and less than 100 acres
5	own more than 100 acres
11,298	

The making and maturing of sparkling Champagne is a very highly skilled and costly business beyond the means of some ten thousand *vignerons:* they grow grapes and sell them to a comparatively small number of wealthy concerns, or "Shippers", who have immense cellars where millions of bottles of sparkling Champagne are prepared and matured to be sold eventually in all parts of the civilised world through a network of highly paid agents.

CHAPTER FIVE

Côtes du Rhône

THE RHÔNE has no sooner risen from its icy cradle than its long run from Alpine snows to the blue waters of the Mediterranean starts among vines, those of the highest vineyards in Europe from Visp to Zermatt: their Heidenwein and Gletscher, or Glacier wines, are Rhône wines, but not *Côtes du Rhône* any more than the wines of Savoie and Bugey along the valley of the Rhône, from its entry into France until it joins the Saône at Lyons.

There are some very pleasant Savoie and Bugey wines, most welcoming and attractive when you call upon them, but poor travellers. Some of them, such as La Côte Grèle, once Brillat-Savarin's own vineyard at Valromey, and Mont-mélian, between Chambéry and Saint-Jean-de-Maurienne; the Coteaux de Crépy, south of the Lake of Geneva; Talloires, Thonon, Ayse, and at a number of other places, the white wines enjoy a greater measure of popular favour than the red wines; there is also a sparkling white *Seyssel* and a sparkling *rosé Chautagne* in great demand locally, but none of these are Côtes du Rhône wines.

The greatest characteristic of the true Rhône wines are their essential stability and keeping quality. Bred from vines grown in inches of soil on stony, steep, terraced slopes, these wines have good colour and a distinctive *bouquet*: they will last for years without loss of either. A Rhône wine is often not bottled until five years old, and usually in burgundy-shaped bottles, sometimes with a conceit of thin silver wire netting round them, quite charming and infinitely useless.

The Côte du Rhône wines are wines from grapes grown on either bank of the Rhône along the 125 miles of its run from Lyons to Avignon. The Côtes du Rhône wines vary greatly in style and quality, and they may be divided as follows:

1. Côte Rôtie
2. Condrieu
3. Hermitage
4. Saint-Péray
5. Châteauneuf-du-Pape
6. Tavel

Côte Rôtie

Côte Rôtie is the northernmost of the Côtes du Rhône vineyards and it produces the finest red Côtes du Rhône wine. The name is given to a range of hills, barely two miles in length, on the right bank of the Rhône, in the Commune of Ampuis-Côte-Rôtie, about five miles from Vienne on the opposite bank of the river. The *vignerons* of Ampuis claim that their vineyards date back to A.D. 600 and, if so, it is remarkable that the soil shows as yet no sign of being exhausted: on the contrary, it brings forth finer red wines than any of the other Rhône valley vineyards where the same black grape, the *Syrah*, locally known as *Sérine* or *Serène*, is cultivated.

A stony bluff that rises screen-like behind the little town of Ampuis-Côte-Rôtie is known as *Côte Brune*, and another immediately to the south of it, is called *Côte Blonde*, on account of the greater proportion of lime in its soil. The terraced vineyards of both the *Côte Brune* and *Côte Blonde* produce the finest of the red wines of the Rhône, those of the *Côte Brune* possessing rather greater breed and being regarded as the better of the two. To be entitled to the name of *Côte Rôtie*, the wines of both the *Côte Brune* and the *Côte Blonde* must have an alcoholic strength of at least 10°, and they must be made from at least 80% of *Syrah* or *Sérine* grapes.

Condrieu

A little farther south, where the Département of the Rhône ends and the Département of Loire begins, the vineyards of Condrieu are partly in the Commune of Condrieu (Rhône) and partly in the two adjoining Communes of Vérin and Saint-Michel-sous-Condrieu (Loire). The only grape grown is the *Voignier*, a white grape from which a golden wine of very fine quality is made but, unfortunately, in very small quantities only. The few acres of Condrieu vineyards are shared among 17 different owners, and the finest vineyard of all, 2.47 acres only, known as Château Grillet, is the property of a Monsieur Neyret-Cachet; the quality of its wine is superlative. It is one of the very best white wines of France. The alcoholic strength of the white wines of Condrieu and Château Grillet is never inferior to 11°.

Hermitage

Rising sharply, pyramid-like, from a broad base to a height of a thousand feet, the Hermitage Hill towers over the sleepy little town of Tain-L'Hermitage sprawling along the left bank of the Rhône, opposite Tournon. The Hermitage Hill occupies a commanding position, yet there are no ruins of any fortress nor traces of ancient fortifications: there is, however, a small chapel built upon the site of the vineyard given, in 1225, to a returning Crusader Knight turned Hermit, Henri de Sterimberg.

These sloping friendly vineyards should be visited during the *vendange* when men with great tubs of grapes on their backs descend to the waiting carts with the agility of mountain goats, although it is not advisable to get in their way. The picture of grey stone, blue sky and the bright clothing of the *vendangeurs'* is unique and unforgettable.

From Tain-L'Hermitage to St. Christopher's Chapel, near the brow of the Hill, and a little distance beyond, there are 346 acres of vines cultivated in the folds of the Hill: they produce on an average 55,000 gallons of wine every year, about two-thirds of it red wine, from the black Syrah grape, and the rest white wine from Roussanne and/or Marsanne grapes. Both the red and white wines of Hermitage possess vinosity and breed, as well as an attractive *bouquet* faintly reminiscent of honeysuckle.

The vineyards of Crozes-L'Hermitage, close to those of the Hermitage Hill, towards the south-west, produce on an average 12,000 gallons of wine, mostly red, similar to the wines of Hermitage.

Upon the opposite side of the Rhône, in the Ardèche Département, beyond Tournon and immediately north of Saint-Péray, the vineyards of Cornas produce a fair amount of red wines similar in character to those of Hermitage but with more body and greater alcoholic strength, 11° instead of 10°.5 (Cornas) and 10° (Hermitage).

Saint-Péray

Saint-Péray is an old-world little town basking in the sun, on the right bank of the Rhône opposite Valence; it is hemmed in on all sides by vineyards which have produced during many centuries past red and white wines of high repute. Today, the red wines of Saint-Péray are consumed locally and anonymously, the *Appellation Contrôlée* "Saint-Péray" being exclusively reserved for the white wines, still and sparkling. These white wines are made from Roussanne and/or Marsanne white grapes, but, owing to differences in the nature and depth of the soil, they produce much lighter wines at Saint-Péray than they do upon the other side of the Rhône, up on the Hermitage Hill.

Ever since the year 1829, when some sparkling wine was made at the Château de Beauregard, near Saint-Péray, a good deal of the white wines of Saint-Péray are handled in the same manner as is Champagne and rendered sparkling.

Châteauneuf-du-Pape

When the Popes lived at Avignon some five centuries ago, they probably had a summer residence built here, but it is likely that vines were cultivated long before. The name is romantic and has perhaps helped the wine, which it hardly needs, if for no other reason than its alcoholic strength, which is appreciably higher than that of most other French red wines.

The vineyards which produce the red, *rosés* and white wines of Châteauneuf-du-Pape stretch across what was many centuries ago probably the crater of an extinct volcano. Their soil must be fertile since it produces a great deal more grapes than all the other vineyards of the Côte du Rhône put together, and yet it is entirely covered up by a relentless tide of shingle, pebbles and stones of various shapes, colours and sizes. Planted apparently haphazard, but may be according to some carefully thought-out plan, there are different varieties of grapes, all growing together, mostly the Syrah, Grenache, Clairette, Mourvèdre, Picpoul, Terret noir, Coudoise, Muscadin, Vaccarèse, Picardan, Cinsault and Gamay *noir à jus blanc*, for the red wines. The white grapes grown for the making of white wines are chiefly the Roussette, Marsanne, Bourboulenc, Carignan, Pinot *blanc de Bourgogne*, Viognier, Pascal *blanc* and Mauzac. The warmth and power which all good Châteauneuf-du-Pape wines possess in a greater measure than all other French table wines is due to the fact that both red and white wines are made from about fourteen different species of grapes, as well as to the greater force of the summer sun than in either the Côte d'Or or the Gironde. The mini-

Plate 17   CHAMPAGNE. The wine and the glass. The first Champagne bottles had a somewhat longer and narrower neck than those in general use today, as may be seen by the bottle in this picture. The superbly graceful glasses shown were specially designed for the French Champagne Shippers Association to display the unique properties of their wine: glorious colour and *bouquet* with the bubbles rising in the glass until the last drops. A feature of Champagne is the many-coloured metal foils in which shippers dress the bottles—to each his own.

mum alcohol strength of both the red and the white wines of Châteauneuf-du-Pape is 12.5°.

The best wines of Châteauneuf-du-Pape are those sold under the names of individual vineyards, estates or firms such as the Châteaux Fortia, de la Nerthe, Vaudieu, La Gardine, the Cru Saint-Patrice, the Clos de L'Oratoire des Papes, etc.

The white wine of Châteauneuf-du-Pape possesses a darker shade of gold than most white Burgundy wines, often also more body but its *bouquet* is usually very discreet.

Tavel

Roquemaure, opposite Châteauneuf-du-Pape, was once a busy port from which Languedoc wines were shipped not only to Lyons and Paris but to England and Holland. Thus, in 1744, there were 12,000 hogsheads of wine loaded at Roque-maure, and there is every reason to believe that most of it came from the vineyards of Tavel and Lirac, immediately to the west of Roquemaure, or those of Chusclan, to the north, in the valley of La Cèze, a tributary of the Rhône.

Although there are late eighteenth and early nineteenth century "Wine Labels" bearing the names of Roquemaure and Chusclan, none is known that bears the name of Tavel. Yet, today, the wines of Chusclan, Roquemaure and Lirac are all sold merely as *Côtes du Rhône*, whereas the wines of Tavel have their own *Appellation Contrôlée*, in France, and they enjoy all over the world a greater measure of popularity than all other *vins rosés*. The soil of the Tavel vineyards is nought but sand, lime and loose flints: how vines can grow – nay flourish – in such baked and barren ground must be seen to be believed, and yet their grapes yield a *vin rosé* that possesses both charm and a great deal more power than they are given credit for by unwary drinkers.

The *vignerons* of Tavel make their famous *rosés* in many ways and some use as many as four or five different kinds of grapes. Two white grapes and two red is a common prescription in set and ordered proportions. Thus there is a great variation in Tavel wines which at their best are quite delicious and have more essential character than any other *rosés*. (See special note on *rosé* in glossary.)

Plate 18 A RHÔNE VALLEY GRAPE. The *Syrrah*. Especially suitable for growing on the steep, sunbaked rock escarpments of the Rhône Valley, the Syrrah grape is responsible for the clean, heady, red wine of Hermitage and the Côtes du Rhône. These grapes photographed at Tain-L'Hermitage are ready for the press; the skins are beginning to wrinkle in the hot sun of early autumn.

CHAPTER SIX

Loire

T HE WINES OF THE LOIRE and its tributaries are made in one of
the most beautiful parts of France, and one of the most interesting of the
French vine-growing districts. Almost everywhere along the course of
this long and gracious river from Blois to Saint-Nazaire the scenery is
magnificent, a vast panorama of wooded and vine-clad hills, great châteaux and
venerable cities. Lovely as are the vineyards of Burgundy, Alsace and the Rhône
valley, those of the Loire have greater breadth and majesty. The same cannot
be said, however, of the Loire wines, many of them quite charming, some of
them very fine, but none of them great wines. Comparatively few of the Loire
wines are sold under the name of the *vigneron* or his château but mostly under the
Appellation Contrôlée of the district, village, and, sometimes, the vineyard responsible for the wine in the bottle. Bad vintages are the exception in the
Loire Valley so that less importance attaches to the date of different vintages
than is the case for other French wines; many of the Loire wines are sold without any vintage date, and most of them are best when young.

The Loire is the greatest of the great rivers of France. It rises in the Cévennes
Highlands and flows from south to north as far as Orléans, where it turns
sharply to the west, passing through Blois, Tours and Nantes before reaching
the Atlantic opposite Saint-Nazaire, after a 625 miles' far-from-straight run. The
Loire crosses twelve Départements with an aggregate of over 500,000 acres of
vineyards, and those which produce the more popular Loire wines are the Nièvre, the Cher, the Indre-et-Loire, the Maine-et-Loire and the Loire Inférieure.

The Upper Loire

Nièvre

There are many vineyards all along the Loire before the river comes to Nevers, but none of them bring forth any wines of real merit until we come to those of the Nièvre Département. The vineyards of the Nièvre which produce the best and better-known wines are those of Pouilly-sur-Loire, a busy little market town on the right bank of the Loire about half-way between La Charité-sur-Loire and Cosne. The wines of Pouilly-sur-Loire are mostly white wines and there are two quite distinct sorts known, the first and much the best as *Blanc Fumé de Pouilly* or *Pouilly Fumé*, and the other, a much cheaper wine, which is simply called *Pouilly-sur-Loire*. The *Blanc Fumé de Pouilly* or *Pouilly Fumé* is a white wine which must not be below 11° in alcoholic strength, and it must be made entirely from Sauvignon grapes, grapes which are exactly the same as the Sauvignon of the Gironde but they are better known in the Upper Loire by the name of *Blanc Fumé*. The plain *Pouilly-sur-Loire* wines, on the other hand, are made from Chasselas grapes and their alcoholic strength may not be below 9.5°. They are not merely lighter wines, but they have not got the peculiarly attractive gunflint *bouquet* which the Sauvignon grapes, grown in these Upper Loire vineyards, imparts to the *Blanc Fumé* wines. Both white wines, however, must come from the vineyards of Pouilly-sur-Loire or those of the adjoining Communes of Saint-Andelain, Tracy-sur-Loire, Saint-Martin, Saint-Laurent-sur-Nohain, Garchy, and Mesves-sur-Loire. Of course, all the better wines add to *Pouilly Fumé* the name of their own Château or vineyard. There is but one Château in the district, Château du Nozet, but there are a number of particularly good vineyards, such as Les Loges, Les Côtes Rôties, Les Nues, Les Vourigny, Les Foletières, and Les Chantalouettes.

Cher

Upon the other bank of the Loire, in the Cher Département, almost opposite Pouilly-sur-Loire but a little farther north, the vineyards of the Sancerre district are more extensive and bring forth a great deal of very attractive white wines, produced also from Sauvignon grapes, wines which are very similar to the *Blanc Fumé de Pouilly*, but, as a rule, lighter than the best white wines of Pouilly-sur-Loire. To be entitled to the *Appellation Contrôlée* "Sancerre", their alcoholic strength must not be below 10.5°. The only wine-producing Château of the Sancerre district is the Château de Sancerre, and the white wines of the Sancerrois which are reputed the best are those of Chavignol.

Some distance to the south-west of Sancerre, but still in the Cher Département, there are some very attractive, light white wines, with a distinctive *bouquet* of their own, made from the vineyards of Quincy, which overflow into the neighbouring Commune of Brinay. These vineyards, about 550 acres in all, occupy a fairly high tableland on the left of the river Cher. They are planted with Sauvignons, the noble white grape which, according to tradition, was first introduced to Quincy by the Cistercian Monks, in the fifteenth century, when the nearby Abbey of Beauvoir was built. To be entitled to be sold under the name of Quincy, the white wines of the Quincy vineyards must not be inferior to 10°. in alcoholic strength.

Touraine

Indre-et-Loire

The Département of Indre-et-Loire corresponds to the greater part of what was, until 1790, the Province of Touraine. Its chief city is Tours, the capital of Touraine from Gallo-Roman times, and the vineyards which grace both banks of the Loire, as it twists and turns on its wayward way from east to west, across Touraine, produce a great deal of very nice wines, both white and red, still and sparkling.

White Wines: All the better white wines of Touraine are made from a white grape from Anjou called *Chenin blanc* in Anjou, but more commonly known as *Pinot de la Loire* in Touraine, although it has none of the characteristics of the Burgundian Pinots. Other white grapes grown in Touraine vineyards are the *Meslier du Gâtinais*, and the *Sauvignon du Bordelais;* also the *Folle Blanche des Charentes*, to a very much smaller extent. The best and best-known white wines of Touraine are the still and sparkling wines of Vouvray. The vineyards of Vouvray are perched on the top of some lime cliffs, which are honeycombed with the cellars and living quarters of many *vignerons*, facing the right bank of the river Loire on one side and the valley of the little river Cissé on the other. They stretch from above Tours to Noizay, in two Communes west and two east of Vouvray, i.e. Sainte-Radegonde, Rochecorbon, Vouvray, Vernon and Noizay, on the Loire, as well as the two Communes of Chançay and Reugny, in the Cissé valley.

All Chenin blanc wines from any of those Communes are entitled to the use of the name of Vouvray when their alcoholic strength is not inferior to 11° for the still wines, or 9.5° for the sparkling varieties. The better wines of Vouvray bear the name of their native vineyard as well as that of Vouvray, such as Clos Moncontour, the wine of Château Moncontour; Clos Le Mont, owned by Messrs. Ackerman Lawrance; Château Gaudrelle, owned by J. M. Monmousseau; Clos Paradis, owned by Ch. Vavasseur; all in the Commune of Vouvray. Also Clos de la Taisserie and Clos Chevrier, at Rochecorbon; Clos de la Halletière, at Sainte-Radegonde; Clos L'Hermineau and Château de l'Etoile, at Vernon-sur-Brenne.

Facing Vouvray, upon the left bank of the Loire, Montlouis, half-way between Amboise and Tours, is the centre of extensive vineyards, some of them, which face the Loire, are planted with Chenin blanc and produce white wines of the Vouvray type, but lighter in alcoholic strength, whilst the vineyards upon the other side of the hills, facing the Cher valley, are planted in Breton and Côt black grapes, and produce red wines.

Upstream from Montlouis, the vineyards of Saint-Martin-le-Beau and farther east those of Lussault, in the Amboise Canton, produce some very attractive but light white wines. Other vineyards of the Amboise Canton, more particularly those of Nazelles, on the right bank of the Loire, produce very nice white wines but not great.

South and south-west of Tours, the vineyards of the Indre Valley produce some most acceptable Chenin blanc white wines, the best of them being those of Artannes, Azay-le-Rideau, Cheillé, Saché and Vallères, near the Loire; and those of Perrasson, Saint-Jean-Saint-Germain, and Sepmes, a good deal farther up the Indre Valley, beyond Loches.

The generally accepted practice in Touraine is to bottle white wines when about six months old and to let them age in bottles rather than in cask. To do this, however, the wine must be both bright and safe at the time of bottling; to be bright the wine has to be fined and it may even be filtered as well; to be safe from any further fermentation, it may also be *bisulfité*, a chemical process that renders impossible any further yeast activity.

Red Wines: All the better red wines of Touraine are made from the *Cabernet franc* grape which was brought to Touraine many years ago by one Abbé Breton, and ever since the Cabernet franc has been known in Touraine as Le Breton. The Malbec grape, another Bordelais grape, is also to be found in Touraine vineyards, more particularly those of the Cher valley, but its local name is Côt instead of Malbec. Other black grapes grown to a very much smaller extent here and there are the Pinot noirien of Burgundy, called Plant Meunier or Plant noble, the Grolleau and the Gamay.

All the better red wines of Touraine come from two main districts, one is Rabelais' own country, the *pays Véron*, Chinon and the Vienne valley on the left bank of the Loire; and the other the Bourgueil uplands, upon the right bank of the Loire.

Chinon

There are red, *rosé* and white wines made from grapes grown upon both banks of the river Vienne on its last lap before joining the Loire at Candes. The best, however, are the red wines, which have a very attractive violet-scented *bouquet* and greater elegance than power: their alcoholic strength rarely exceeds 10° and it must not be below 9.5° to be entitled to the *Appellation Contrôlée* "Chinon". Chinon itself and its vineyards are upon the right bank of the Vienne. The best growths are La Vauzelle, Rochette-Saint-Jean, Les Clozeaux, La Rochelle, and Saint-Louans.

Downstream from Chinon, in the stretch of country between the right bank of the Vienne and the left bank of the Loire, known to Rabelais as *Le Pays Véron*, the best red wines are those from the vineyards of Beaumont-en-Véron: among their best growths, mention should be made of La Roche Honneur, Château de Danzay and Les Pouilles.

Upstream from Chinon, and upon the left bank of the Vienne, the best red wines are those from the vineyards of Ligré, and among their best growths are Saut-aux-Loups, La Noblaie, Les Roches-Saint-Paul and Le Vau Breton.

Bourgueil

Bourgueil red and *rosés* wines have an obvious family likeness to those of Chinon across the Loire, but they are generally more masculine, that is of rather bigger frame and more assertive, even if not actually of greater alcoholic strength, although they often are a little stronger: their *bouquet* is more reminiscent of the raspberry than the violet. The red wines of Bourgueil cannot be fairly described as better than those of Chinon, but they are certainly better-known, which is due to the fact that there is a great deal more red Bourgueil than there is red Chinon. The red wines entitled to the name of Bourgueil must not be below 9.5° in alcoholic strength and they must be made from Breton (i.e. Cabernet franc) grapes from Bourgueil vineyards. The *Appellations Contrôlées* authorities recognise as "Bourgueil" vineyards, besides those of Bourgueil itself and of the adjoining Commune of Saint-Nicolas-de Bourgueil, all others upon a fairly high tableland rising from the right bank of the Loire, at the western limit of the Indre-et-Loire Département, and overflowing into the Maine-et-Loire Département, that is, from west to east, the Communes of Benais, Restigné, La Chapelle-sur-Loire, Ingrandes, and as far as Saint-Patrice. All the best red Bourgueil wines come from either the higher ground vineyards of all these Communes, known as *Côtes*, or those pockets of sandy gravel at lower levels known locally as *Graviers*. Some of the more popular of the *Côtes Bourgueils* are Le Clos de la Gardière and Le Clos de la Turellière, Saint-Nicolas-de Bourgueil; Le Grand Clos and Le Clos des Perrières, Bourgueil; La Chevalerie and Les Brosses, Restigné. Among the best of the *Graviers* wines, mention should be made of the following: Le Clos du Fondis and Le Clos de la Chevalerie, Saint-Nicolas-de Bourgueil; Le Clos de la Salpètrerie and Le Clos de l'Abbaye, Bourgueil; Le Clos Jollinet and Le Clos de la Plâtrerie, Restigné.

The red wines of Touraine are made from black grapes picked when fully ripe, crushed or mangled and usually *égrappés* before being pressed in order to get most, if not all, of the red colouring matter from the inner lining of the grape skins. The must is left to ferment in an open vat for about eighteen hours after it leaves the press; by then, it should have got rid of all the dirt and dust that came in with the grapes, and it is drawn clear into the casks in which fermentation will be carried out to its completion at a progressively slower and slower rate. As a rule, the red wines of Touraine are ready for bottling two years from the date of the vintage, but they are generally bottled in their third year.

Anjou

Anjou, the cradle of the Plantagenet dynasty, between Touraine in the east and Brittany in the west, ceased to be a Province in 1790, when most of it was included in the present Maine-et-Loire Département, with Angers as its chief city and the Loire as its main river, which divides it into two sections of about the same importance, north and south.

The vineyards of Anjou which produce the greater quantity of wine, mostly white wines, both still and sparkling, are those of the southern half, or left bank of the Loire; those responsible for the best wines are the vineyards of Saumur and those of the Coteaux du Layon and Coteaux de l'Aubance, two of the many tributaries of the Loire. The northern half vineyards are responsible for a great deal of wine, but there is only a little of it of real merit, although many are charming.

Saumur

Saumur is by far the most universally known of all Anjou wines: this is due to the commercial publicity responsible for the world-wide demand which sparkling Saumur has long enjoyed. Sparkling Saumur either under its own or one of its many *noms de guerre*, is made, it is claimed, in exactly the same way as Champagne, and this may well be true, but it is not Champagne; it is sparkling Saumur, a good, clean, rather sweet sparkling wine considerably handicapped by having to pay the same heavy duty as Champagne. No Loire or Anjou still wine would claim the peculiar attributes of the great wines of Burgundy or Bordeaux nor can its sparkling wines those of Champagne. There are, however, much greater quantities of still wines than sparkling wines made from the Saumur vineyards: some are red, and their alcoholic strength must not be below 10° to be entitled to bear the name of *Saumur;* more are white and others are *rosés*, the minimum alcoholic strength of the whites being 9.5° and that of the *rosés* 9°. All the better white wines are made from the Chenin blanc grape, the original Plant d'Anjou which was adopted in nearby Touraine but renamed Pinot de la Loire. The more *ordinaires* white wines are made from commoner species of grapes, chiefly the Muscadet, also called Melon, and Gamay blanc, a Burgundian grape; or else the Folle blanche, Blanc Emery and Groslot blanc. All the best red wines are made from Breton, i.e. Cabernet franc, grapes, or Chenin rouge, which is also called Pineau d'Aunis; the more *ordinaires* red wines are mostly made from Gamay grapes, and *rosés* from Groslot grapes.

The vineyards of the Saumur hillsides are very extensive; they stretch from the leftbank of the Loire, immediately west of the Touraine boundary southwards, to the boundaries of the Maine-et-Loire Département, covering the Communes of Bagneux, Bizay, Brézé, Brossay, Courchamps, Coutures, Cizay-la-Madeleine, Dampierre-sur-Loire, Douces, Douée-la-Fontaine, Fontevrault-l'Abbaye, Meigne-sur-Doué, Saint-Cyr-en Bourg, Rou-Marson, Montreuil-Bellay, Montsoreau, Parnay, Puy-Notre-Dame, Saint-Hilaire-Saint-Florent, Saumur, Soulanger, Souzay-Champigny, Turquant, Les Ulmes, Varrains, Le Vaudelnay.

Coteaux du Layon

Whilst the white sparkling wines are the best know wines of Anjou, the sweet white wines of the Coteaux du Layon are acknowledged to be wines of finer quality than any of the many white wines of the Loire Valley. They are made from Chenin blanc grapes, picked as late as possible, when fully ripe or overripe, from the vineyards of 28 Communes of the valley of the river Layon, one of the Loire's tributaries. The best vineyards are in the Communes of Thouarcé-Bonnezeaux, Faye, Rablay, Beaulieu, Saint-Aubin-de-Luigné, and Rochefort-sur-Loire. Of all the different growths of these and other Layon Communes, none is more famous, and none deserves its fame more fully, than the Quarts de Chaume (Rochefort-sur-Loire). Other popular growths are the Clos de la Roche Gaudrie and Château de la Roche (Rablay); Château de Montbenault (Faye); La Guillaumerie (Rochefort-sur-Loire); La Saulaie and La Haie Longue, and Château Fresnaye (Saint-Aubin-de Luigné); La Petite Croix and Château de Fesle (Thouarcé-Bonnezeaux).

The Lower Loire

Coteaux de la Loire

Upon the right bank of the Loire, at no great distance south-south-west of Angers, the vineyards of the Coteaux de la Loire produce much white wine of no great distinction, as well as a comparatively small quantity of very nice still white wines from the Coulée-de-Serrant and La Roche-aux-Moines, the two best vineyards of the Commune of Savennières. They are not so sweet as the wines of the Layon, across the Loire, but they have breed and charm as well as a distinctive and attractive *bouquet*.

Muscadet

Muscadet is the name of a white Burgundian grape which was renamed Muscadet when it was introduced into Brittany, where it has now practically ceased to be cultivated, except in the Département of Loire Inférieure, north of the Loire, round about Ancenis close to the border of Anjou; also south of the Loire, to the east and south-east of Nantes. *Muscadet* is also the name of the white wine made from the Muscadet grape, a light, fairly dry white wine, with little *bouquet* and a faint "squeeze of lemon" sharpness which makes it most acceptable with Marennes oysters, *saucisson* and any vinegary hors d'oeuvre.

Muscadet is not a wine to lay down. It is at its best when young and lively, usually before it reaches its third year. As a wine it is too thin and hungry ever to be popular in England, where, however, it had many admirers during the eighteenth century, but in its distilled form. It used to be shipped from Nantes and called Nantz or Nancy Brandy, and there was quite a brisk demand for it, a demand which, particularly during the periods of war, was chiefly supplied by flourishing fraternities of smugglers.

CHAPTER SEVEN

Alsace

ALSACE IS THAT LONG TRACT of beautiful and fertile land that stretches from below Mulhouse, just north of Switzerland, to beyond Strasbourg, as far as the German Palatinate. It is protected from western gales by the high range of the Vosges mountains and, less effectively, from cold winds and worse from the East by the Rhine. Between the Rhine and the Vosges, the river Ill flows parallel to the Rhine for many miles before it joins it near Strasbourg. This river, the Elsus of the Romans and Elsass of the Germans, has given its name to Alsace, and it more or less divides the land lengthwise into plough and grass on its right, or Rhine side, and wine and timber on its left, or Vosges side. There are a number of small rivers twisting and bending, rushing and cascading down from the Vosges to join the Ill, and they have carved for themselves in the course of the centuries their way through the foothills of the great Vosges mountains wherever their waters found and eventually broke down lime and schist patches, more yielding than the all-pervading granite. Which is how and why there are so many and such beautiful little valleys in Alsace with vineyards thriving upon the lower half, from 75 to 300 feet, rarely higher than 600 feet, along the slopes of the hills, which are mostly thickly wooded higher up, and dominated at a short distance to the west by the 3,000 feet high peaks of the Vosges.

The wines of Alsace were very little known, if at all, before the end of the First World War, and the end of the seventy-seven years of the German occupation of Alsace. But long before this period, there were vineyards in Alsace and there were wines of Alsace drunk in Alsace and sent down the Rhine to the North Sea, Scandinavia and England. A thousand years, almost to the day, before that fatal war of 1870, Alsace was handed to King Louis of Germany, at the Treaty of Verdun in 870, a decisive factor being that without Alsace, Louis would have been without wine. In 1300, there were 172 villages named as being responsible for the best wines of Alsace, but all through the Middle Ages and down to the end of the eighteenth century, many of the Alsatian vineyards, and all the better ones, belonged either to the Church or to some great feudal lord. As late as 1790, when the French Revolution brought about the crash of the old order, the Rangen hill, near Thann, which had been famous for its wines for centuries, was still the property of the Strasbourg Cathedral; the Clos In der Wanneri, near Guebwiller, belonged to Murbach Abbey; the best Bergheim vineyards to the Knights of St. John; those of Sigolsheim hill to the Ebersmunster Abbey; large vineyards at Alspach and Kaysersberg to the Counts of Alspach and Remiremont; and the best vineyards of Turckheim to the Abbey of Munster.

In Alsace, just as at Vougeot, Carbonnieux and Hautvillers, to name but three of the more famous Benedictine-blessed bacchic foundations, wine was made to the glory of God, as good as it could be made by men of goodwill. For many centuries, labour was serf or near-slave labour, and money was not nearly as important as a good name, and what surer road to a good name is there than good wine? There were no hotels in those days, and no hospitals other than the guest-houses for wandering scholars and hospitals for the sick built, staffed and run by the Church, which is why the Church had in Alsace perhaps more than elsewhere many vineyards, and as a rule the best.

After the French Revolution and the Napoleonic wars, the big estates in Alsace were broken up, and the vineyards were sold to a very large number of peasant owners, whose great-grandchildren own the same vineyards, but divided again and again and now smaller than ever. Alsace itself was divided, like all French Provinces, into two smaller Départements, the Haut-Rhin and Bas-Rhin, Upper and Lower Rhine, the first with Mulhouse and Colmar as its two chief cities; the second with Strasbourg, the proud capital of old Alsace. Most of the best vineyards of Alsace are in the Haut-Rhin, from Thann, in the south, to Sigolsheim in the north, and from the Vosges in the west to the Ill Valley in the east. Among the better known, pride of place must be given to Riquewihr and Ribeauvillé, two of the most picturesque and unspoilt villages, but Guebwiller, Eguisheim, Turckheim, Ammerschwihr, Hunawihr, Bergheim and others have very fine vineyards, even if most of them were less fortunate in the Second World War than Riquewihr.

The vineyards of the Bas-Rhin, from below Sélestat in the south to Hague-nau beyond Strasbourg, in the north, are mostly in the plain and produce commoner types of wines for local consumption. There are, however, in the Bas-Rhin some hillside vineyards which produce excellent white wines, such as the vineyards of Mittelbergheim, Barr, Obernai and Kintzheim.

In the long and chequered history of Alsace, the nineteenth century has an exceptionally black record. To start with, the quality of the wine was no longer what it had been for so long: all the smallholders who had for the first time wine of their own to drink and to sell were far too keen to make as much wine – and money, from their few acres of vines, and they planted the commoner species of grapes, pruned them "long" instead of short, and gathered far bigger crops of grapes than ever before – but, of course, they made inferior wine. Then, after the Napoleonic wars, came the tariff war between France and the German States. There were so many better wines made in other parts of France at the time, that there was little demand for Alsace wines; on the other hand, the German States taxed all French wines out of their territories as a reprisal for the taxation of German produce in France. Oïdium in the '50's and phylloxera in the 1870's were scourges which all vineyards had to suffer during the nineteenth century, but all were spared the tragedy of German occupation which blighted the Alsatian vineyards from 1870 to 1918. The main purpose of the German authorities during that period was quite obviously to eradicate as much as possible every-thing that was French, in order to germanise Alsace and its people; wine was unfortunately one of the first victims. Its identity was ruled out by the prohi-bition to offer it for sale under the name of Alsace wine; its quality was lowered by the permission to blend it with 49% of any kind of wine; its production was rendered unprofitable by the encouragement given to the manufacture of arti-ficial wines and their sale at prices very much below that of the cheapest genuine Alsatian wines. Which explains why it was that nobody ever heard of any Als-atian wine before the end of the German occupation of Alsace, in November 1918. Since then much has been done to bring back the better species of grapes in the Alsatian vineyards as the first condition for the making of good wine.

The Vines

The vines which are cultivated in the vineyards of Alsace are mostly of the commoner sorts: Elbing, Burger, Knipperlé and Trollinger, which are responsi-ble for nearly two-thirds of the vinous production of Alsace: the wines made from these species are sharp, when young, and as they are mostly drunk within eighteen months of their vintage, they are sharp when drunk by the people of Alsace. They are not made for export and suitable only for home consumption: pickled and fermented cabbage *(chou rouge et choucroûte)* as well as every part of the pig, roast, boiled, stewed, pickled, or smoked, being the basic diet of the bulk of the Alsace people, a young and acid wine has a most beneficial splitting and moving quality.

All the better white wines of Alsace, roughly speaking a third of its total vinous production, are made from Sylvaner, Muscat, Pinot, Riesling, Traminer and Gewurztraminer grapes.

Sylvaner

Sylvaner is a more popular grape in the Bas-Rhin vineyards than in those of the Haut-Rhin. The white wines made from Sylvaner grapes are light, elegant, pleasant and fresh, when young, but they have little *bouquet* and they do not repay keeping; it is the best value, as a rule, among the less expensive wines.

Muscat

Muscat, of which there are three different varieties, is very different from the white muscat grapes grown in glasshouses. It has quite a highly developed *bouquet* which leads one to expect a wine with more body and of finer quality than most Alsatian Muscat wines possess: they usually lack breed or distinction and are somewhat earthy.

Pinot

Pinot is another species of grape of which there are two distinct varieties: *Pinot blanc* and *Pinot gris*. The first is known also as *Weissklevener* or *Burgenberg*, and the second as *Rutlander* or *Tokay*. The white wines made from both these grapes have less *bouquet* than a Muscat-made wine, but more body and greater distinction.

Riesling

Riesling is a noble grape, one which is grown to a far greater extent than any other in the vineyards of Ribeauvillé, Riquewihr and Hunawihr, as well as in the choicest positions of all good vineyards. The Riesling is a late-maturing grape which makes it all the more important to give it a more sheltered place than to hardier species. The white wines made from Riesling grapes possess both the *bouquet* and body which entitle them to a place in the front rank of the fine white table wines.

Traminer and Gewurztraminer

Traminer and *Gewurztraminer* are two names for the same grape, a noble grape, smaller and rounder than the Riesling. The great advantage which the Traminer has over the Riesling is that its fruit sets and ripens earlier; this is important because when the weather happens to deteriorate in early autumn, Rieslings are picked before they are quite ripe whilst Traminer, gathered at the same time, will be ripe and will give a better wine. If, on the other hand, the sun shines and the weather is all that one could wish it to be, Rieslings will be gathered fully ripe and their wine will be excellent, and the Traminer grapes may be left when they have come to the ripe stage, to become overripe, through the *pourriture noble*, as happens at Yquem; the wine made from such *Trockenbeerenauslese*, or simply late gathered grapes will produce a wonderful dessert wine, luscious and delicious, the peer of the great Sauternes and Palatinate dessert wines.

There are very few large Estates in Alsace but a very large number of small-holders with just enough grapes to make from two to ten casks of wine, too little to go to the expense and trouble of marketing their wine. They sell it either to a Co-operative Society of their own, or to one of the wine-merchants who have cellars at home to mature the wine and agents abroad to sell it. In both cases, the wine which the grower sells is sold simply under the name of the grape from which it was made, either Sylvaner, Riesling, Traminer, and so on. The name of the actual grower does not matter any more than the name of his vineyard or village: all that the *Caves Co-opératives* or the Wine Shippers want to know is the *Cépage* or grape variety so as to make their blends of Sylvaners, Rieslings or Traminers. These, when ready for sale, will be sold under the name of one of those grapes, with the name of the Shipper added as well as his address. There are, however, a few of the more progressive shippers of Alsatian wines who do make wine from one species of grape, grown in one single vineyard, such as the Clos du Maquisard, shipped by Messrs Dopff and Irion, of the Château de Riquewihr. Students of both wine and architecture will find the village of Rique-wihr of more than passing interest.

The tendency is for the Alsatian *vigneron* to spare no trouble to make better wines and to produce some of a finer type for export, comparable to the more delicate wines of the Moselle. It will of course take time, but the start has been made.

There are according to official statistics, 440 wine-producing parishes in Alsace and 30,000 families of *vignerons*. The figures of wine-producing vary greatly: the highest on record being 1,678,400 hectolitres in 1875, and the lowest 121,469 hectolitres in 1917. 15,000,000 gallons would appear to be a fair average, two-thirds of it being consumed in Alsace and one-third being either sold in Paris or exported.

CHAPTER EIGHT

Other French Wines

Arbois

ARBOIS IS AN old and charming little town nestling in a bower of vines, half-way between Salins and Poligny, at the northern end of a long and narrow strip of vineyards facing south-west and with the fir-clad Juras immediately behind them.

There are five different types of wines entitled to the *Appellation Contrôlée* "Arbois":

(1) red and *rosés* table wines made from Poulsard and Trousseau grapes;

(2) white table wines, made from Chardonnay and Savagnin blanc grapes;

(3) *vin jaune*, made from Savagnin grapes exclusively, fermented according to a special technique and matured for not less than six years before being offered for sale;

(4) *vin de paille*, a white wine made from overripe Savagnin grapes, picked in November and even early December. It is fermented sherrywise so that it is quite dry, of high alcoholic strength, and it will keep and improve for a great many years;

(5) sparkling wines made according to the *méthode Champenoise*.

There are other Jura wines and the best are those of L'Etoile. There are also

Plate 19 THE VIN ROSÉ OF ANJOU. The charming wines of Anjou, usually white or rosés, are made in the Département of Maine-et-Loire. The photograph shows an early Anjou wine bottle with its modern equivalent with pale rose-coloured wine in the traditional glasses, not used elsewhere in France.

finer *Vins jaunes* and *Vins de paille* than those of Arbois; they are those of Château-Chalon, the name not of a Castle but of a cluster of vineyards between Ménétru and Voiteur.

Provence

Between Marseilles and Toulon, along the Mediterranean seaboard or southernmost part of Provence, there are many vineyards which produce much wine from middling to fine in quality.

Nearer Marseilles, the little fisherfolk village of Cassis has given its name to the wines from vineyards that crown the cliffs of the adjoining *Calanques*, those fiords of the Mediterranean. The vineyards of Cassis cover 675 acres, but there is not much more than a third of them planted with the shy-bearing old species of Provence grapes, which yield the only wines entitled to the *Appellation Contrôlée* "Cassis". Most Cassis wines, and all the better ones, are white wines.

Nearer Toulon, there are vineyards at La Gaude, Saint-Tropez, La Croix de Cavalaire, Cagnes and elsewhere which are responsible for red wines of fair quality, but the best-known and best of them are those of Bandol, a small port where, they say, ships used to load, in days of long ago, wines for London, Rotterdam and Bremen. None but the wines from the vineyards of Bandol and a few nearby Communes are entitled to the *Appellation Contrôlée* "Bandol".

Near Nice the red, white and *rosés* wines of Bellet are the best-known of the *Alpes Maritimes Département* wines.

Languedoc and Roussillon

Languedoc is the name given to an immense tract of land stretching roughly from the Rhône below Lyons to the Garonne above Toulouse, from east to west, and from the Forez in the north to the Mediterranean Sea in the south. The Roussillon, a much smaller Province, is wedged between Languedoc and Spain, north and south, with the Comté de Foix to the west and the Mediterranean Sea to the east. That long stretch of Mediterranean seaboard from Marseilles to the Pyrénées and the Franco-Spanish frontier has been for centuries past, and still is, the home of the Muscat grape, and all the best dessert wines of France come from the coastal vineyards of Languedoc (Lunel and Frontignan) and Roussillon (Banyuls, Maury, Rivesaltes, Côte d'Agly, and Côtes du Haut-Roussillon).

Plate 20 AN ANJOU GRAPE. The *Chenin blanc*. The Chenin blanc thrives on hills and slopes beside the Loire and its many tributaries: it is responsible for some of the finest of the charming and delicious wines made in Anjou, wines which are ready when quite young but do not stand the test of time or improve with age as the Pinot-made wines of Burgundy and Champagne.

Both Lunel, some 15 miles north-east of Montpellier, and Frontignan, about 12 miles to the south-west of the same city, on the road to Sète, are in the Hérault Département. The only wines which are entitled to the *Appellation Contrôlée* "Muscat de Lunel" are wines with an alcoholic strength not inferior to 15°, made exclusively from Muscat grapes from the vineyards of Lunel, Lunel-Viel, and Vérorgues.

Frontignan is a slightly fortified wine with a minimum alcoholic strength of 15°, made exclusively from Muscat grapes from the vineyards of Frontignan and of the adjoining Commune of Vic-la-Gardiolle.

When we come to Rousillon, we are in the land of the *Vins doux naturels*, the unfortified sweet dessert wines with a minimum alcoholic strength of 14°, which is obtained through the slow and thorough fermentation of very sweet grapes, mostly Muscats.

From the Spanish frontier to Argelès-sur-Mer, there are four Communes along what is locally known as La Côte Vermeille, i.e. Cerbère, Banyuls, Port-Vendres and Collioure, which produce the sweet white, red and *rosés* wines entitled to the name of *Banyuls*. Banyuls is unsweetened as well as unfortified, but it is sweet and of higher alcoholic strength than any table wines simply because it is made from grapes so ripe and so rich that after reaching the optimum alcoholic strength through fermentation, they still retain some unfermented sugar. This applies, of course, not only to the wines of Banyuls but to all the *Vins doux naturels* of Roussillon.

Maury is a village farther away from the sea and higher up upon the foothills of the Pyrénées: it is surrounded by vineyards which, according to local tradition, were first planted in the year 277 B.C. by some of Hannibal's soldiers turned *vignerons*! The *vins doux naturels* of Maury owe their characteristic *bouquet* to the *Grenache noir*, which is the local grape from which they are made.

Rivesaltes, nearer the sea, on the road from Narbonne (35 m. north) to Perpignan (5 m. south) was the birthplace of Maréchal Joffre. Its vineyards, and those of the nearby Communes entitled to sell their wines as *Rivesaltes* (Salses, Fitou, Leucate, Baixas, Pia, etc.) grow mostly Muscats but some Malvoisie grapes as well.

Côte d'Agly

"Côte d'Agly" is also an *Appellation Contrôlée* for the *vins doux naturels* made from Muscat, Grenache and Malvoisie grapes from the vineyards of the Agly Valley, between Rivesaltes, to the east, and Maury, to the west. The largest vineyard of the Agly Valley is that of Château de Caladroy (250 acres). Tautavel,

Estagel, Cases de Pène, Vingrau, and Espoira-de-l'Agly are the five more important of the eleven Communes entitled to sell their wines under the name of Côte d'Agly, to which is usually added *Muscat*, *Grenache* or *Malvoisie*, according to the particular sort of grape from which the wine was made.

Côtes du Haut-Roussillon

"Côtes du Haut-Roussillon" is an *Appellation Contrôlée* for the *vins doux naturels* made from Muscat, Grenache and Malvoisie grapes grown in the vineyards of the highlands immediately behind Banyuls, facing the sea from Perpignan to the Pyrénées and the Spanish frontier immediately to the south. The more important of the wine-producing Communes of the Haut-Roussillon are Argelès, Cabestany, Canet, Castelnou, Fourques, Laroque-des-Albères, Le Boulou, Llupia, Passa, Perpignan, Pollestres, Ponteilla, Saleilles, Sainte-Colombe, Saint-Jean-Zasseille, Saint-Jean-Pla-de-Cors, Saint-Genis-des-Fontaines, Saint-Nazaire, Sorède, Terrats, Thuir, Tordères, Tresserres, Trouillas, Villeneuve-de-la-Roho, and Villemolaque.

Gaillac

Besides the *vins doux naturels*, there are both still table wines and sparkling wines made in Roussillon, Languedoc and other vineyards of the south-west, chief among them the wines of Gaillac, Limoux, Monbazillac, Bergerac, Montravel and Jurançon.

Gaillac, 14 miles from Albi and 35 miles from Toulouse, in the Tarn Département, is in Languedoc; it is built on the river Tarn and its vineyards produce a great deal of wines, both still and sparkling, the best of them being those from Mauzac grapes, grown upon granite on the left bank of the Tarn. They possess a distinctive and pleasing gunflint aftertaste which is completely lacking in the wines made from the same species of grapes grown on limestone upon the right bank of the Tarn.

Limoux

Limoux, in the Aude Département, in Roussillon, some 15 miles from Carcassonne, is chiefly noted for its sparkling white wine, made according to the Champagne *méthode* and known as *Blanquette de Limoux*. It has plenty of gas in it and it is fairly sweet.

Monbazillac, Montravel

Monbazillac might be called the Sauternes of the Dordogne. It is made from Sauvignon and Muscadelle grapes, which are picked when they have reached the stage of *pourriture noble;* it is darker than most Sauternes, tinged with red, fuller of body, sweet, and its *bouquet* is rather more assertive, but it has not the same *finesse.*

The vineyards of Monbazillac and of the four Communes entitled to the *Appellation Contrôlée* "Monbazillac" face the Dordogne, about as far south from Bergerac as the Sauternes vineyards are from Langon and the Garonne. Opposite, upon the right bank of the Dordogne, the vineyards of Bergerac and those of Montravel immediately to the west produce much white wine and a little red wine.

Jurançon

Jurançon, just south of Pau, and the Communes entitled to the same *Appellation Contrôlée*, produce the finest white wine of Béarn and Bigorre, a full strength wine of real distinction; it has a puzzling *bouquet* with a truffle-like quality which is unique. Jurançon is usually kept in cask for some years before being bottled and it improves greatly with bottle-age. The grapes from which Jurançon is made are Béarn species – *Petit* and *Gros Manseng* and *Courbu,* which are not grown anywhere else.

Other French Wines

There are not hundreds but thousands of other French wines, millions of gallons of *Vins du Midi* and other mostly homely or plain wines, which are wholesome and helpful, thirst-quenching and stimulating, but without any claim to "breed", *bouquet* or distinction of any kind. There are also quite a number of very nice wines made in all parts of France, but in such small quantities that they are rarely, if ever, available to anybody other than the people who make them, and their own friends.

In my opinion, neither the mass-produced wines for the masses nor the totally uncommercial wines, however good they may be, deserve a place in this recording of the Noble Grapes and the Great Wines of France.

CHAPTER NINE

Brandy

SPIRITS HAVE BEEN DISTILLED from fermented liquids ever since man found out that there is less heat needed for alcohol than for water to reach boiling point, that is when a liquid becomes a gas or vapour. This difference makes it possible to remove by the right degree of heat some or most of the alcohol present in fermented liquids. There are in all of them, besides alcohol, various by-products of fermentation, small quantities of which are distilled off with the alcohol. These by-products owe their importance to the fact that they are generally characteristic of the material subjected to fermentation, such as wine, sugar-cane, molasses, barley-mash, etc., and they give to brandy, rum, whisky and other spirits their individuality and appeal. But when spirits are distilled from potatoes, like Vodka, or from cellulose, like some of the Swedish Akvavit, their by-products are undesirable and they are removed by further distillation or 'rectification'.

Spirits therefore differ according to:

(1) the origin and nature of the fermented liquids from which they are distilled;
(2) the degree and manner of their distillation;
(3) whether or not rectified after distillation;
(4) if matured in casks, and for how long.

Brandy is the anglicized form of the Dutch *Brantjwyn*, burnt wine, a more matter of fact name than the French *Eau de vie*, water of life.

121

Brandy is a spirit distilled from wine, anywhere. It has been and it is distilled in most if not all lands where grapes grow and wine is made. There are wines, however, far more suitable than others for distillation, and there are very few indeed that have in their gift brandy of unchallenged excellence. There are, roughly speaking, ten casks of a new white table wine "burnt" or distilled to secure one cask of brandy, a wasteful process unless the brandy obtained at such a cost be good enough to command a price at the very least ten times greater than that of the wine from which it was distilled.

The types, styles, qualities and prices of brandy differ greatly and this is due chiefly to:

(a) the wines from which brandy is distilled;
(b) the manner of its distillation;
(c) the skill and the stocks of the blender;
(d) the casks in which the brandy is matured, the humidity of the cellar where it is kept, and the length of time during which it is kept in cask.

Cognac

Between Brittany and Gascony, south of the Loire and north of the Gironde, there is a much more modest river, but one that is just as famous in the annals of gastronomy, La Charente. On its leisurely roundabout way from up-country to the Atlantic, the Charente passes through three of the smaller former French Provinces, Angoumois, Aunis and Saintonge, corresponding roughly to the Upper (Angoulême), Middle (Cognac) and Lower (Saintonge) reaches of the river. These three small Provinces became, in 1790, two large Départements, La Charente and La Charente Inférieure: the latter, however, after the fall of France, in 1940, could not abide being "Lower" or *Inférieure* any longer and changed its name to La Charente Maritime. Cognac is the name that no Brandy may be given other than the Brandy distilled from wine made from grapes grown within the boundaries of those two Départements, as well as a very few and quite un-important acres in two of the adjoining Départements.

Cognac, the town which has given its name to the finest Brandy in the world, is 312 miles from Paris, 32 from Angoulême and 16 from Saintes. Built upon the right bank of the Charente some two thousand years ago, Cognac was a busy river port long before anybody had ever thought of distilling Brandy, actively engaged for centuries in two branches of commerce concerned with salt and wine, both basic necessities of life. Salt came from Saintonge to Cognac, where it was stored and sent eventually by barge as far as Angoulême, and thence by road further inland. Wine came from Aunis and Angoumois to Cognac to be stored and sold presently to overseas merchants, and then shipped by river and by sea from La Rochelle to England, Flanders, the Hanseatic cities and the Baltic ports. There is, however, no documentary evidence available today of the existence of any vineyards in the immediate vicinity of Cognac before the year 1031, when Robert Le Pieux gave to the Priory of Saint-Léger the undulating plain that slopes from the little hill where Merpins stands today, a modest village but a fortified camp in the days of Caesar and the Roman occupation – at the junction of the little river Né and the Charente, down to the outskirts of Cognac, some three and a half miles away. The monks who cultivated the land, planted a vineyard in that loop of the Charente which is to this day the very heart of La Grande Champagne. There is no lack of evidence of the activity of the wine trade of Cognac from the twelfth to the sixteenth century. Thus, in 1214, King John, whose wife was the daughter of the Count of Angoulême, commissioned the *Prud'hommes* or Elders of Cognac to buy Aunis wines for the royal cellars. There are many records not merely of the royal favour but of the popularity of the wines of Aunis in England, Lubeck, Flanders and Denmark, up to the sixteenth century when civil war utterly ruined viticulture and brought commerce to an end. Nowhere else in France was the fratricidal feud between Catholics and Protestants more bitter and disastrous, no pitched battle more bloody than the battle of Jarnac, in 1569. When at long last, in 1596, the Edict of Nantes brought in some hope of greater tolerance and peace, houses had to be rebuilt and vineyards replanted. Whether different and unsuitable species of grapes were chosen at the time or whether the *vignerons* who had survived massacres and escaped being burnt at the stake had lost the art of making wine as good as their fathers made, we may never know, but what we do know is that the wines of Aunis, Saintonge and Angoumois practically ceased to be shipped during the seventeenth century. Available records leave no doubt as to the reason for this; there is nought but complaints about the bad quality of these wines, and more particularly about their unsuitability for shipment by sea. One cannot help thinking that the wines which were such bad travellers could not have been the same as those which had been shipped from La Rochelle for so long, to everybody's satisfaction, in former times. However, necessity being the mother of invention, the people of Cognac and thereabouts who could no longer sell their wines as wines were not long in discovering a new way of disposing of them under another form, as brandy.

The art of distillation was well known in France during the sixteenth century, when liqueurs and brandies were distilled and compounded by apothecaries and alchemists, and prescribed by doctors only. By the middle of the seventeenth century, however, liqueur compounding had become one of the privileges and accomplishments of the perfect housewife, whilst the distillation and sale of brandy had become a branch of the wine trade. It was then that the undoubted superiority of the brandy distilled from the wines of the Charentes became known outside the Cognac country. Ever since, Charentes white wines have had no particular merit as wines, but when distilled they are responsible for brandy of exceptional excellence.

Cognac brandy is distilled at the beginning of the year, during the winter months following the vintage, as soon as the new wine has finished fermenting and has "fallen bright". It is distilled from white wine, wine made from different varieties of white grapes, chiefly from a grape oddly named *Saint-Emilion*. It is very similar to, if not actually the same as the Italian *Trebbiano* grape. All grapes from which white wine is made to be distilled into Cognac brandy must grow within the strictly defined boundaries of the Cognac area, roughly speaking the two Départements of Charente and Charente Maritime. There are, of course, within those two Départements, marked geological differences in the soil of their vineyards which means that different qualities of brandy are distilled from the wine of different vineyards. All the finest Cognac brandies are distilled from the wines of vineyards nearer to Cognac, in one or the other of three areas the soil of which is the richest in lime. The best of the three is known as *Grande Champagne*, the next best is called *Petite Champagne* and the third *Borderies*. Farther east, where the soil is quite different, vineyards have replaced forests and those areas are still called *Bois – Fins Bois, Bons Bois, Bois éloignés;* the brandies distilled from the *Bois* areas have not got the finesse nor the breed of *Champagnes* and *Borderies* Cognacs, but they are nevertheless true Cognac brandies and brandies of good quality.

There are twenty-one Communes in the *Grande Champagne* area, all in the *Arrondissement* of Cognac, mostly between Cognac, Ségonzac and Châteauneuf. There are fifty-five Communes in the *Petite Champagne* area in the *Arrondissements* of Cognac, Jonzac, Barbezieux and Saintes. In the *Borderies*, there are only eight Communes and they are all in the Canton of Cognac.

Cognac brandy is always distilled in pot stills. A pot still is a copper pot with a broad rounded bottom and a long tapering neck to which is attached a copper spiral tube or worm condenser. The wine is put in the pot; it is slowly brought to boiling point and kept simmering; the wine rises from the pot in the form of vapours which are condensed into liquid form by the time they reach the con-denser. The spirit collected from the first vapours to leave the pot are called the "head": the last are the "tail"; the head is too pungent, the tail not enough; both are drawn off and not mixed with the "heart", that is the spirit distilled in-between, which alone deserves to bear the name of Cognac.

There are in the true Cognac district over 4,000 *vignerons* who distil their owe wine themselves, but very few of them have either the capital or the cellarage needed to keep the brandy they distil until it is fit to drink. The majority of the *vignerons* sell their newly distilled brandies to one or the other of the great shipping houses possessing besides the means of holding large stocks of brandy, a world-wide distributing organisation for its sale.

The Cognac shipper may and often does own some vineyards and distil his wine, but he also must buy newly distilled brandy from some of the 4,000 *vginerons* of the Charentes, in order to build up and keep up ample stocks of brandy of different ages, quality and price, from different vineyards and different vintages.

The more important and the more varied the Shipper's stocks of brandy are, the easier it is for him to ensure the continuity of style of the different brandies which he sells under various marks or brands. This is important because the consumer who calls for his favourite brand of brandy expects that it will be true to type, that it will look and taste "the same as before".

Good brandy must be given time to show how good it can be, and as it needs a fair amount of oxygen to bring forth the aldehydes and esters responsible for its delightful fragrance, it must be matured in casks. The casks must be perfectly sound and well seasoned; brandy would immediately acquire a fusty smell should a single stave be musty. A sound cask gives to the brandy matured in it a little colour; also a characteristic and softer "finish".

Brandy in cask will mature differently if kept in a dry or in a damp place; the drier the store or warehouse, the greater will be the evaporation, so that the brandy will lose more bulk and less strength. In a damp vault or cellar, brandy will lose more strength and less bulk; it will hydrate itself or incorporate some of the hydrogen of the humid air, a better method than adding distilled water to it.

The finest brandies may gain by being kept as long as thirty or even forty years in cask, but most brandies are at their best long before, and there is no greater, nor any more popular fallacy, than to imagine that the older a brandy is the better it must be.

The climatic conditions prevailing in the Charentes are such that there are marked differences in the quality of the brandies distilled each year, in good and bad vintages. The brandies of all good vintages are but very rarely sold as Vintage brandy, as they are indispensable for making up the Cognac shippers' various blends.

There is, however, much Cognac brandy that is sold in bottles that bear a date, which most buyers take for granted to be the date of the vintage of the brandy in the bottle. But it is not always so. Sometimes, it represents the age of the oldest brandy, a little of which was used in making the blend, but it may also bear no relation whatever to the age of the brandy in the bottle; it may be used merely for the sake of the selling value of an easily remembered date, such as 1066 or 1865; such dates may have been used merely as an indication that the brandy in the bottle is quite old enough to be enjoyed without waiting any longer. Napoleon brandies upon the bottles of which are sometimes branded such dates as 1811 or 1815 are not for men of little faith. There *may* be such wonderful brandies, but *would* they be so wonderful?

There is some vintage Cognac brandy which it is sometimes possible to buy in England; it is that which was imported in cask immediately after it was distilled within about six months of the date of the vintage, lodged in bond on arrival, and left alone until bottled years after. This is always a rare and often a very fine brandy, and it is to be sought after.

A liqueur brandy may be, quite exceptionally, a matured brandy of some particularly fine vintage, but as a rule, it is a blend of different brandies, all of respectable origin and may be some of illustrious pedigree, which have been matured for a number of years in casks.

It has long been the practice of many important Cognac shipping houses to give some indication of the age of their liqueur brandies by using the following initials:

V.S.O.   (very superior old), for brandies from 12 to 17 years old;
V.S.O.P.   (very superior old pale) for brandies from 18 to 25 years old;
V.V.S.O.P.   (very, very superior old pale), for brandies from 25 to 40 years old.

Liqueur brandy need not be very old, but old enough nevertheless to be mellow and fragrant. It is the best of all liqueurs to be sniffed and sipped at leisure after a good dinner: it also possesses the most valuable medicinal and therapeutic properties.

Liqueur brandy is called in France *Fine Champagne*, or *Fine Maison*, "the brandy of the house", which is sometimes surprisingly good.

Armagnac

Next to Cognac, Armagnac is the best brandy distilled in France. Of course, a good Armagnac is better than a poor Cognac, but in general the finest Armagnac is not so fine as the finest Cognac.

The Armagnac vineyards cover approximately 125,000 acres widely scattered in the Gers, Landes and Lot-et-Garonne Départements; they are divided into three districts known as Bas-Armagnac, Tenarèze and Haut-Armagnac, the first two being responsible for the finest brandies.

The Armagnac *vigneron* grows mostly *Picpoul* and *Jurançon* grapes, the first being similar to the Cognac *Folle Blanche;* he picks his grapes and makes his wine in October, and distils it in pot stills, as at Cognac, as soon as the fermentation is over; the new spirit is then lodged in casks made of locally grown black oak, which imparts to the brandy, when matured, quite a distinctive character.

There are in the Gers Département some vineyards which produce much better brandies than all others, and it is possible, even if not always easy, to buy the best Armagnac vintages direct from one or other of the owner-distillers or his agent.

CHAPTER TEN

Casks, Bottles & Glasses

Casks

CASKS ARE THE FIRST homes of all wines, their nursery from birth to bottle. Most white wines rarely stay more than a few months in cask, whereas most red wines, and more particularly the better ones, may remain two or three years and even a good deal longer.

French wines are mostly 'lodged' in oaken casks the shape and size of which vary according to different districts. The standard cask, whether called *Fut*, *Barrique* or *Pièce*, never holds much more nor much less than 60 gallons (U.S.A.) or 50.5 gallons (U.K.), which means that it can be shifted about and stacked fairly easily by men who are both strong and skilled. Larger wine containers, whether made of oak or glass-lined cement, *foudres* and *cuves*, are not mobile.

At Bordeaux, wine is sold at so much per *Tonneau* or tun, which is not a cask but the accepted trade unit equal to four *Barriques* or hogsheads. The Bordeaux *barrique* is somewhat squat, fatter and shorter than the Burgundy *pièce* or hogshead. It holds 225 litres of wine, that is 59 gallons (U.S.A.) or 49.786 gallons (U.K.). There are two smaller casks in use in the Gironde, the half *barrique*, which is called a *feuillette* (112 litres) and the quarter *barrique*, which is called a *quartaut* (56 litres).

In Burgundy, the accepted trade unit for the sale of wine is the *feuillette*, in the Chablis district, and the *queue* everywhere else. There is no cask called a *queue*. The name means two *pièces* or hogsheads always sold in pairs. The standard hogshead of Burgundy is known as a *pièce*. In the Côte d'Or, the standard cask is the *pièce de Beaune*, which holds 228 litres (60 gallons U.S.A. or 50.5 gallons U.K.); the *feuillette* and *quartaut* each holds 114 litres and 57 litres respectively. But in the Yonne, white wine is sold by the *feuillette de Chablis*, which holds 172 litres of wine. In the Mâconnais and Beaujolais, at the southern end of Burgundy, the *pièce* holds from 215 to 216 litres, the *feuillette* half and the *quartaut* a quarter of the *pièce*. In the Côtes du Rhône, the *pièce* holds 225 litres, in Champagne 216 litres, in Touraine 225 litres, in Anjou 220 litres, whilst in Alsace the more usual cask used is one that holds 116 litres of wine.

Bottles

Bottles are a more permanent home than the cask for all the better French wines, still or sparkling, Bordeaux, Burgundy and Champagne more particularly; their tenancy varies from three to seven, fourteen, twenty-one years and sometimes even much longer. For the majority of table wines, however, the bottle is merely a convenient container to bring to table a young wine, lately drawn from the cask; once in a bottle, the wine can be easily stored and kept at hand until wanted, whether for a few days or weeks, or for months and years as the case may be.

In France, the standard bottle is the litre (33.81 fluid ounces U.S.A.). Most *ordinaires* wines and all the *très ordinaires* are sold in France in plain, white-glass and full-measure *litre*, *double-litre*, *demi-litre* or in a white glass bottle called *Saint-Galmier*, being the bottle invariably used for the mineral water of that name. The better wines are mostly sold in slightly smaller bottles *(bouteilles)* or half-bottles *(demies* or *chopines)*. Bottles vary slightly in both shape and size, and also in weight. The Champagne bottle is much the heaviest of all, having to be made particularly strong to stand the carbonic gas pressure from within; its shoulders are sloping and its body bigger than that of the Bordeaux bottle, which has more of a 'neck and shoulders'. The standard Burgundy bottle looks very much like the Champagne bottle but it is a good deal lighter, in weight but not colour; there is a slightly smaller Burgundy bottle called *Mâconnaise*. The Alsace bottles are without any shoulders, just long and thin, and green, very similar to the Moselle bottles. The Anjou bottles have long necks and thin bodies. The legal content of various bottles, in France, according to the Law of the 1st January, 1930, are as follows:–

Litres: 100 centilitres
Saint-Galmier: 90 centilitres
Champagne, Burgundy and Rhône bottles: 80 centilitres
Bordeaux and Anjou bottles: 75 centilitres
Fillette d'Anjou and de Touraine: 35 centilitres
Alsace "flute": 72 centilitres

N.B. Post-war Burgundy and Rhône bottles contain 75 centilitres, the same as Bordeaux.

The *Magnum* is a double and the *demie* is a half bottle, hence a *Magnum* of Champagne holds 1.60 litres and a *Magnum* of Claret 1.50 litres: a *demie* of Champagne 40 centilitres and a *demie* of Claret 37.5 centilitres.

Larger bottles are fancy bottles, the contents of which are approximately as follows:–

Tregnum or tappit-hen	3 bottles or 0.525	gallons
Double Magnum	4 bottles or 0.70	gallons
Jeroboam (Champagne)	4 bottles or 0.70	gallons
Rehoboam	6 bottles or 1.05	gallons
Methuselah (Champagne)	8 bottles or 1.40	gallons
Impériale (Claret)	8–9 bottles	

There are also larger bottles called Salmanazar, Balthazar, and Nebuchednezzar, which are supposed to hold 12, 16 and 20 bottles (2.10, 2.80, 3.50 gallons) respectively, but they are not really fit to use as wine bottles; they are monstrosities for show purposes, anybody buying them would deserve to find the wine corked.

All the better quality French wines are now sold in bottles which are fully labelled, but the labelling of wine bottles, in France, is of fairly recent origin. Labels were first used for cordials and liqueurs, many of them home-made, at the beginning of the last century; then they were used for sparkling Champagne and later on for all sorts of wines. Before labels came into general use, bottles were 'dipped': when the cork had been driven in the neck of the bottle, its outside face and a quarter of an inch or half an inch of the neck were dipped into some boiling sealing wax for just one moment; soon after, the wax which had stuck to cork and neck cooled off and became hard, protecting the cork from damp and insects. Wax of many different colours was used, black, yellow and various shades of red, blue and green, and the different wines in the cellar were identified by the colour of their wax-cap, duly recorded in the cellar book or bin book. There were wine-merchants who took a little more trouble and who had steel

1. The Wine and Food Society all-purpose wine glass designed by André L. Simon. The foot is raised, the stem short and the bowl slightly curves inwards.

2, 3, 4. The tulip-shaped Bordeaux, Burgundy and Champagne glasses; flat-footed and long-legged, but elegant, and very slightly pinched at the top.

5. The classical Brandy glass and (6) its big brother; flat-footed and short-legged, distinctly but not excessively incurving.

7, 8. Quite nice-looking little glasses but the wrong shape for the appreciation of wine, owing to the out-curving of the lip.

dyes made to stamp on the wax, whilst still hot, their own name, or the name of the wine in the bottle or the date of its vintage.

There were also wine bottles made to the order of princes or wealthy merchants with their name, initials or arms embossed in the glass of the bottle, usually at the base of the neck, on the 'shoulder'. The best known of those French initialled wine and brandy bottles are stamped with the Napoleonic "N". Some are quite obviously older than the others; hand made, or mouth blown, never absolutely cylindrical, and they must be older than 1815, when the first Napoleon lost all interest in his cellar. The others are machine-made bottles, perfectly cylindrical, and were made from 1850 to 1870, the year when Napoleon III abdicated.

At large Estates, like Château Lafite, for instance, some of the wine was sometimes bottled in the standard Bordeaux bottle but with a 'button' stamped on the bottle's shoulder with the name "Château Lafite" and the year of the wine's vintage, such as 1874. Neither name nor date could be washed or scraped off, which was all to the good, but as the bottle could not be used again for any other wine or vintage, its cost was excessively high. And so the paper label came and it came to stay.

Glasses

Wine glasses can make a very great deal of difference to our enjoyment of wine, which is why they must be chosen with great care. There is no worse mistake than to choose wine glasses as ornaments for the dining-room table, to 'look pretty', not giving as much as a thought to the wine which will fill them. There are some beautiful Salviati glasses with all the colours of the rainbow, and there are some very handsome cut-glass coloured glasses, not unlike old church stained glass, costly and admirable works of art, no doubt, but no good for wine. The first joy that a fine wine has to offer us is its clear, bright, cheerful and beautiful colour, so that the whiter the glass, the better it will be for the wine and for us.

Then there is the size of the wine glass. Wine is not tossed down like Vodka at one gulp, nor is it swilled like foaming beer; wine is drunk without haste and with appreciation. There must not be too much nor too little in the glass. A glass that holds less than 3 fluid ounces is too small: the wine will be cramped in it. But a glass is too large which holds more than 5 fluid ounces. A 4-ounce glass is about the best all-purpose size.

And lastly there is the shape of the glass. There are three French wines with

Plate 21   THE WINE OF ALSACE. Between the Vosges and the Rhine the ancient Alsatian vineyards ripen their many grapes: *Riesling, Traminer* or *Gewurztraminer, Sylvaner, Pinot Gris,* etc. The wines of Alsace are mostly white and often possess great charm and character. They are exported in slender hock-type bottles and served traditionally in long stemmed glasses.

glasses of their own, Champagne, Alsace and Anjou, but quite a number of equally suitable glasses for Bordeaux, Burgundy and the rest. The original Champagne glass was the *Flute* which gives to the wine the maximum number of contacts, hence the greatest amount of *mousse* or bubbles; it was replaced some sixty-odd years ago by the *Coupe*, a flattish saucer on a pedestal, giving the wine the minimum amount of contacts, so that it kept its gas longer but looked rather flat. The *Coupe* was replaced by the *Tulipe*, a much more sensible shape, which the Champagne Syndicat has elongated and enlarged and made into a truly 'de luxe' glass.

Both the Alsace and Anjou glasses are tall glasses but the shape of their bowl is quite distinctive.

Brandy Glasses

The shape and size of brandy glasses depends very much upon the brandy and the occasion.

A tumbler is best for a three-year-old, or One Star brandy, served with a small bottle of cold soda-water, on a hot summer's day.

A *Ballon* or *Tulipe* wine glass of the finest and purest white material and holding half a pint, is large enough for rotating a tot of brandy to coax its *bouquet*, and small enough to be cupped and warmed in the palm of the hand. It is the best glass for a liqueur brandy, and even after the whole of the brandy is gone, such a glass still holds delight for the connoisseur's sensitive and enquiring nose.

It is only when a *nouveau riche* must have "the best", that there is any justification for bringing forth a footed aquarium, without water and goldfish, of course, and making it hot over a spirit-lamp, before pouring in it a few drops of a priceless centenarian brandy, which will lose most of its *bouquet* the moment it comes into contact with the heated glass.

The "bar" and "banquet" midget brandy glasses are a disgrace; they are much too mean to be acceptable at any time.

Plate 22 AN ALSATIAN GRAPE. The *Sylvaner*. The Sylvaner grape is but one of the grapes used by Alsatian *vignerons*, thriving as it does on the lower slopes of the Vosges facing the Rhine: it is not a 'luscious' grape, but produces a wine of pleasing character and fairly light body.

CHAPTER ELEVEN

The Care and Service of Wine

WINE "IN THE WOOD", or in casks, is young wine which needs the care of the expert to complete its fermentation and free itself from all undesirable matter, either vegetal or mineral, such as mucilage and tartar, before being bottled and sold to us to enjoy. As long as a wine is in cask, it is in fairly free contact with the oxygen of the air which is its friend at first but may easily become its worst enemy after a time; this is why wine which is not drunk straight from the cask must be bottled. The amount of air which reaches the wine in a bottle through the cork – a porous substance, but only just – is infinitesimal but by no means negligible: it is probably responsible for the way in which bottled wines improve with age, 'probably' because the behaviour of bottled wines has as yet never been explained to the satisfaction of scientists.

What is quite certain, however, is that bottled wine must be given a decent home to live in until wanted. A cellar, or failing a cellar, a cupboard, bin or a shelf, which is to house bottled wine, must be as free as possible from variations of temperature. If we bear in mind that heat expands and that cold contracts, we shall easily realise that changes from heat to cold and cold to heat will 'tire' any wine in a bottle. Although we do not know very much about the 'ageing' process of wine, we do know that unless it be given complete rest and darkness, in a place free from draughts, vibrations, and even noises, a cool place for choice,

134

wine will go sick or flat or dumb. If one has no proper place to keep wine in one's home, it is far better not to have more than just enough for day to day or week to week requirements: one's wine merchant will always oblige, in town, and keep one's wines properly, delivering small quantities as and when wanted. Of course, if we live in the country, we ought to have a cellar of our own, underground, facing north, away from the central heating boiler; a cold, dark, dry, quiet, and clean cellar where wine may be left with every chance of improving. A dry cellar is more easily kept clean and free from mouldiness than a damp cellar, but a damp cellar is not necessarily a bad cellar; cork weevils do not like damp cellars.

Of course, every bottle of wine that is "put down" in cellar or cellarette, in bin or on shelf, must be laid in a horizontal position so that the wine in the bottle be at all times in contact with the inside face of the cork.

When the time comes to "pull a cork", the metal capsule on bottles of still wine must be cut below the ring of the bottle-neck, and not merely flush with the cork. The capsule is made of lead and is treated chemically to protect the cork: it stinks. The wine, as it is poured out, should not come into contact with the cut metal capsule, and the only way to make sure of this is to remove the capsule altogether, or to cut it below the ring which is there to catch and divert any drops of wine. Once the capsule has been cut below the ring, the neck of the bottle should be thoroughly wiped. The cork should then be drawn and the inside lip of the bottle wiped with a clean cloth. Drive the corkscrew slowly right through the centre of the cork and draw the cork steadily without any jerks, without haste or hesitation.

Generally speaking, clarets and ports of almost any age should be decanted, and so should all Burgundies of more than ten years old. Any red wine will look better in a clear crystal decanter especially if decanted with care. Decanting is a simple enough operation particularly if a wicker cradle is used for the purpose of carrying the bottle from the bin to the table, and as a receptacle for holding the bottle firmly whilst the cork is drawn, and the mouth and neck of the bottle wiped clean. The wine should then be decanted by holding the bottle (not in the cradle) in the right hand over a lighted candle in a darkened room. The flame of the candle should be just below the shoulder of the bottle, and decanting should stop when the sediment, or crust, begins to run into the neck. The result should be a perfectly clear ruby liquid with all the sediment left in the bottle. Cradles used for serving at table are mainly used in restaurants for the flattery of customers who should know better. The constant ebb and flow of pouring will muddy the wine except it be a Beaujolais or light burgundy, which can then be poured straight from the bottle without any chi-chi. When decanted, the cork can be allowed to lie across the mouth of the decanter both as an indication

of the contents and to impede the entrance of foreign bodies like midges who
are also wine-lovers.

Sometimes a cork breaks in the neck of the bottle, especially with very old
wine, and here the wine cradle is very useful; it allows you to probe with your
corkscrew, much as a dentist will deal with your teeth, once you are firmly
placed in his chair. With experience most broken corks can be removed cleanly,
but if all fails and pieces of cork reach the wine, decant the wine through a fine
mesh tea strainer if you do not possess a wine strainer. Decanting magnums
and larger bottles is a more difficult process, but it is always possible to find
some kind of a box to act as a cradle.

Corkscrews must *always* be of the 'cut' edge type, not of the 'round' wire type,
and the great secret is to be sure to screw them well in. Most good shippers now
use the so-called 'long' cork which may be all of a couple of inches long.

Very old wine should not be decanted until just before serving, others from
two to three hours before the meal. There is however no rule about this; some
wines keep longer than others, but generally if a wine is more than, say thirty
years old, there is a risk of fast fading once the bottle is opened.

Temperature

The temperature of the wine at the time of serving is of very great importance
but it is impossible to lay down any cast-iron rules. So much depends upon the
wines themselves, the food served with them, and climatic conditions.

One may, however, accept it as a general rule that all white wines are better
served cold, and red wines at the temperature of the dining room. But cold does
not mean frozen. Wine that is too cold either numbs or burns the tongue and
palate, so that it is quite impossible to appreciate any *finesse* or charm which the
wine possessed originally.

For the wine connoisseur, no white wine should be colder than fifty degrees;
but tea addicts, whose tongues are coated with tannin, and gin addicts, whose
palates are pickled or seared, prefer their wine colder.

Red wines, and more particularly old red wines, are best *chambrés*. This does
not mean 'hotted-up', but brought gradually to the temperature of the dining
room – that of an average London or Paris dining-room, about sixty degrees.
Never, for fear that it might be too cold, plunge a bottle of red wine in hot water
or place it in front of a fire. It is much better to serve a red wine too cold than
too warm. If it is too cold it can always be nursed in the palms of the hands to
raise its temperature; if it is too warm, it is past all human help.

CHAPTER TWELVE

The Art of Making Wine

WINE-MAKING IS AN ART which the genius of man discovered at the dawn of the world's history; it has largely contributed to the well-being of mankind and to the growth of all arts ever since. The distinctive character of every wine is due principally to the species of grapes from which it is made; to the geographical situation and to the geological formation of the vineyards where those grapes are grown; and to the more or less favourable weather conditions prevailing each year. But the striking differences which exist between various kinds of wines, either dark or light in colour; still or sparkling; sweet or dry; are due to the manner and degree in which they are fermented, and to the way they are treated during and after fermentation, or, in other words, to different methods of vinification.

The art of wine-making comprises three principal stages: (1) the crushing of the ripe grapes to obtain their juice; (2) the fermenting of the must to obtain wine; and (3) the maturing of the wine either in cask or bottle, constantly and carefully watching it and attending to it, before it is ready for consumption.

Whilst various processes of vinification obtain in different wine-producing districts, there is one all-important factor in the art of wine-making which is common to all, viz., fermentation.

137

Fermentation

Fermentation consists in a series of complex chemical changes, the most important of which causes the transformation of grape-sugar into ethyl alcohol and carbonic acid gas, a transformation which is rendered possible chiefly by the accelerating or catalystic action of the fermenting enzyme known as Zymase. But grape-juice is not a mixture of water and grape-sugar with saccharomycetes in it. It is very complex, and there are in it other enzymes besides Zymase. There are other chemical reactions taking place at the same time as those which are responsible for the presence of ethyl alcohol in wine, and these different reactions depend, in the first place, upon the chemical composition of the must, and the presence of certain enzymes – and, in the second place, upon external conditions existing at the time.

Climatic conditions are beyond the control of man. The soil of the vineyards may be improved to a certain extent by drainage and fertilizers, but its chief characteristics remain unaltered. Species of grapes may be judiciously selected and grafted. Grapes may be carefully picked and they may be pressed by different methods, but the last stage, the fermenting of grape-juice into wine, which is so important, may be controlled by the art of man more than any of the other factors which are responsible for the making of wine.

Different processes of fermentation are suited to the different chemical composition of different "musts", and their aim is to secure different types of wine.

On the whole, it may be said that the process of fermentation, which is an absolutely natural phenomenon, might be left to transform grape-juice into wine without any interference from man, except in the case of sparkling, fortified, or other such wines. This is true, but like all truths, it is true only up to a point. Grass grows in the fields quite naturally, even in wet fields, but, if no one attends to ditching and hedging, moss may some day grow quite naturally where clover used to grow. Wine left too long to ferment upon its husks will draw colour from the skins if they be those of black grapes, but it will also draw from the pips, stalks or the small pedoncules, more acidity and tannin and more of the unsuitable acids which may prove objectionable later.

Alcoholic Fermentation

Let us measure a gallon of grape-juice and weigh the quantity of grape-sugar it contains. Say that we find 32 oz. of grape-sugar present. Then let us look for our 32 oz. of sugar after the same grape-juice shall have finished fermenting. We shall not find any sugar but, in its place, we shall find about 17 oz. of ethyl alcohol. What has happened? This. Each molecule of grape-sugar, representing 180 by weight, has been split up by fermentation into two molecules of ethyl alcohol (each 46 by weight) and two molecules of carbon dioxide (each 44 by weight). The carbon dioxide has lost itself in the air and the ethyl alcohol has remained in the wine – hence a gallon of wine will be lighter than a gallon of grape-juice, the difference being that of the weight of the escaped carbonic acid gas. At the same time, 17 oz. of ethyl alcohol take up the same space as 32 oz. of grape-sugar, so that we shall have a gallon of wine in place of a gallon of grape-juice, the bulk of our wine being practically the same as the bulk of the grape-juice, although its weight will be slightly less.

We could, therefore, describe alcoholic fermentation by means of the following simple formula:–

$$C_6H_{12}O_6 \quad = \quad 2C_2H_6O \quad + \quad 2CO_2$$

(Grape-sugar)   (Alcohol)   (Carbon dioxide)

Remembering that the atomic weight of carbon, hydrogen and oxygen are respectively: $C = 12$; $H = 1$; $O = 16$; one molecule of grape-sugar, two of ethyl alcohol and two of carbon dioxide will represent:–

(Grape-sugar)	*(Alcohol)*
$C_6 = 12 \times 6 = 72$	$C_4 = 12 \times 4 = 48$
$H_{12} = 1 \times 12 = 12$	$H_{12} = 1 \times 12 = 12$
$O_6 = 16 \times 6 = 96$	$O_2 = 16 \times 2 = 32$
180	92

(Carbon dioxide)

$$C_2 = 12 \times 2 = 24$$
$$O_4 = 16 \times 4 = 64$$
$$88$$

Alcoholic fermentation is therefore a molecular re-adjustment of the carbon, hydrogen and oxygen of grape-sugar. In theory, it seems quite simple – in practice it is very complicated.

To begin with, grape-sugar is not a compact entity made up of six atoms of carbon, twelve of hydrogen and six of oxygen. On balance, there is that number of atoms to be found in one molecule of grape-sugar, but they are arranged in distinct groups in the following manner:–

$$
\begin{array}{ccc}
\textit{Dextrose} & & \textit{Fructose} \\
CHO & & CH_2OH \\
| & & | \\
CHOH & & CO \\
| & & | \\
CHOH & + & CHOH \\
| & & | \\
CHOH & & CHOH \\
| & & | \\
CHOH & & CHOH \\
| & & | \\
CH_2OH & & CH_2OH \\
\end{array}
$$

There are 6 atoms of carbon, 12 of hydrogen, and 6 of oxygen in their grouping; they are knit together in a strictly orderly manner, until the saccharomycetes give the signal, by a loud rap on the piano, for a wild game of musical chairs. Then all is confusion, order is destroyed, there is a rush, hot pursuit, until, all of a sudden, the music ceases and order reigns once more. Some have lost their seats, others have changed seats and have new neighbours. Of course, if there is no air in the room there cannot be any game. This is a very rough and unscientific simile, but it may serve to convey to the mind the main idea of alcoholic fermentation; it necessitates someone at the piano, i.e. an enzyme; it begins and ends with order, but the intervening period is very confused, and it is during this confusion that all sorts of things happen. There is a loss incurred in the process, and, above all, oxygen, i.e. fresh air, is wanted all the time.

Although Zymase, the fermenting enzyme, is necessary to the process of alcoholic fermentation, it does not take any active part in the game which it sets going. Its chemical composition is such that it acts as a catalyst, that is to say a remover of hindrance or an accelerator of reactions. It does so without taking anything away or giving up any of its own substance.

Temperature and Fermentation

A suitable temperature for the immediate growth of the saccharomycetes is of great importance, since their enzyme "Zymase" is indispensable to alcoholic fermentation. But wine is not merely grape-juice with its grape-sugar changed into alcohol and carbon dioxide: in grape-juice there are many other substances besides grape-sugar, and they cannot be expected to remain unaffected by the internal revolution which destroys the chemical structure of grape-sugar and rebuilds with the same materials, ethyl alcohol and carbon dioxide. This revolution is the work of alcoholic fermentation, but other fermentations take place at the same time, other vegetable substances which were in grape-juice are altered, increased, reduced or may entirely disappear, in ways which differ according to the different enzymes and other catalysts present, as well as according to differences of temperature affecting not only the rate of molecular exchanges, but also the degree of solubility of certain acids.

Temperature is an important factor in fermentation because of the influence it exercises upon the rate of molecular exchanges and upon the solubility of various acids. Grape-juice is so complex, it contains such a large number of various compounds, that any and every variation of temperature is liable to affect some chemical reaction upon which may depend, at a later date, some characteristic of the wine.

To sum up, let it suffice to say that the process known as fermentation is one which consists mainly in the splitting up of each molecule of grape-sugar present in grape-juice into two molecules of carbon dioxide. But let it be remembered (1) that there are other fermentable substances in grape-juice besides grape-sugar; (2) that, besides Zymase, there are other enzymes as well as other catalysts which render possible subsidiary fermentations which take place concurrently or subsequently, and are responsible for the presence, in wine, of compounds which did not exist in grape-juice.

Wine

Grape-juice is a very complex aqueous solution. Besides water and grape-sugar, it contains acids and other substances, most of them in very small quantities, either of a vegetable or of a mineral origin.

Wine is a still more complex aqueous solution; besides water and ethyl alcohol, it contains glycerine, acids and many substances in minute quantities, some of which never were in grape-juice.

Water and ethyl alcohol form generally about 97 per cent of the volume of wine, but the remaining 3 per cent is made up of very small quantities of a large variety of substances, which vary and give to different wines the distinctive colour, taste and bouquet which are mainly responsible for the charm, or lack of charm, of individual wines.

These substances may be divided into two main groups, one to include all those which were originally present in grape-juice and the other all those which were not.

(1) *Substances, other than water, which are the same in grape-juice and wine:*

> Grape-sugar
> Saccharomycetes
> Some acids
> Cellulose
> Essential oils, mucilage, etc.

(2) *Substances other than ethyl alcohol present in wine, but not in grape-juice:*

> Glycerine
> Other acids
> Alcohols, other than ethyl alcohol
> Esters and aldehydes
> Sundry other substances

(1) Substances, other than water, which are the same in grape-juice and wine:

(a) Grape-sugar

The proportion of grape-sugar which remains in wine after fermentation depends, in the first place, upon the proportion of grape-sugar present in the grape-juice and, in the second, upon the process or method of fermentation resorted to.

In the case of "fortified" or "sweet" wines, whether obtained like Port, by the addition of brandy during fermentation, or, like Sauternes, from over-ripe grapes, the sweeter the grape-juice, the sweeter the wine. But, in the case of beverage wines such as Claret, it is often the reserve.

(b) Saccharomycetes

Although Saccharomycetes are microscopic fungi, there are millions of them and they do not escape in air like carbon dioxide. They remain in suspension in the wine until the end of fermentation or until the proportion of alcohol is such that it arrests their growth. They are so fine and so light that they are neither swept down by finings nor do they fall to the bottom of the cask by their own weight; many are carried down into the lees by the microscopic crystals of cream of tartar to which they adhere, many more lose their identity altogether by reason of the chemical splitting up of their cells, and some remain in the wine for all time.

There is, of course, a very large variety of saccharomycetes and allied members of the vast tribe of yeasts, bacteria and moulds.

A form of yeast-fungi which is not unusual in wines is the Mycoderma Vini, or "flowers of wine". These micro-organisms multiply very rapidly at the surface of wine and remain on the surface in giant colonies, all holding together, and forming a film which can be so complete as to prevent the outside air having any access to the wine. There are quite a number of different species of film-forming microscopic fungi, all of which require much oxygen to grow and all of which grow with astonishing rapidity.

(c) Acids

Generally speaking, the acids which disappear wholly or partly during fermentation are those which are soluble in water and not in alcohol, whilst acids which appear in much larger proportions in wine than in grape-juice are those which are formed by the oxidation of ethyl alcohol.

Let us take but one example of each class, i.e. tartaric acid and acetic acid.

Tartaric acid is the principal acid in grape-juice. It forms a white crystalline salt which is potassium hydrogen tartrate, commonly known as cream of tartar. Cream of tartar is soluble in water but not in alcohol, and a good deal of the cream of tartar in solution in grape-juice becomes solidified in the shape of fine crystals in the presence of the alcohol of wine; in that form, it is heavier than wine, settles in the lees and is left behind when the wine is racked. Cream of tartar is also more soluble in a warm than in a cold aqueous solution, so that if the new wine be kept in a cold cellar, the lower temperature together with the alcohol present will help render a greater proportion of cream of tartar insoluble, thus depriving the wine, after racking, of much acidity present in the grape-juice.

An acid grape-juice does not necessarily ferment into an acid wine. Acidity in grape-juice is of great benefit because it assists the normal growth of yeasts and checks the development of bacteria, so that it is favourable to alcoholic fermentation. If as well as acidity there is a fair proportion of grape-sugar in the grape-juice, this sugar will ferment and be replaced by a fair proportion of alcohol which, in its turn, will cause the crystallisation of a further proportion of cream of tartar, hitherto in solution. In other words, more sugar in the grape-juice means more alcohol in the wine and less cream of tartar. This is easy to prove in Burgundy where Pinot grape-juice and Gamay grape-juice from the same district may be compared: the first contains more acidity and more sugar than the second, but when both have become wine, the first contains more alcohol and less acidity than the second.

Acetic acid in wine is due to the oxidation of ethyl alcohol, one atom of oxygen replacing two of hydrogen, thus:–

$$\text{Ethyl Alcohol} = CH_3CH_2OH$$

$$\text{Acetic Acid} \quad = CH_3CO\ OH$$

The more alcohol there is in a wine and the less oxygen has access to it the smaller will be the quantity of acetic acid formed. This replacement of two hydrogen atoms by one of oxygen is rendered possible by the presence of an enzyme secreted by the schitzomycetes, and they cannot grow without a free supply of oxygen from the air. Hence when "flowers of wine" or other film forming mycoderma cover the surface of wine and prevent all contact with the outside air, no more acetic acid can be formed. On the other hand, wine of a low alcoholic strength kept in a fairly warm place and in contact with the air will soon become vinegar, practically the whole of its ethyl alcohol being changed into acetic acid. Of course, this should be avoided, and it can be avoided with a little care. At the same time, normal and sound wine is seldom free from acetic acid when new and, with time, this acetic acid dissolves certain mineral salts in wine, forming various acetates which are partly responsible for the flavour and bouquet of wine.

(d) Cellulose

Cellulose is a danger in wine because it may fall a prey to certain bacteria which cause its decomposition into fatty acids and carbonic acid gas, the former being particularly objectionable. Decomposed or "fermented" cellulose in red wine is the cause of an extremely light viscous sediment which it is almost impossible to keep out of the decanter and which spoils not only the look but the taste of the wine.

(2) Substances, other than ethyl alcohol, present in wine but not in grape-juice:

These substances are numerous and they vary according to the chemical composition of the grape-juice, the various enzymes or catalysts present, and the rate and mode of fermentation. They consist chiefly of glycerine and other alcohols, various acids, esters and aldehydes.

(a) Glycerine

Most of the sugar in grape-juice is transformed by fermentation into ethyl alcohol and carbon dioxide, but not the whole of it. Pasteur's experiments, which more recent researches have completely confirmed, showed that alcoholic fermentation could not use up more than 95 per cent of the sugar present in grape-juice in the proportion of about 48 per cent ethyl alcohol and 47 carbon dioxide. The remaining 5 per cent of sugar is used up in other ways; a small quantity being used by saccharomycetes themselves by way of food or means of cellular development; a small percentage being decomposed into minute quantities of various volatile acids and the greater proportion being used up in the production of glycerine.

(b) Other Alcohols

Besides glycerine which, after and a long way behind ethyl alcohol, is the most important by-product of vinous fermentation, there are other alcohols in wine. Such are propyl and butyl alcohols, practically in all cases, and amyl alcohol sometimes. Although these and other alcohols are present in normal wines only in minute quantities, they have, like all alcohols, the property of forming esters with acids, and they play quite an important part, compared to their volume, in the formation of the bouquet or aroma of wine.

(c) Acids

Some of the acidity in the grape-juice, particularly in the shape of cream of tartar, disappears during fermentation, but on the other hand, there are some acids which were not in the grape-juice and which are normally present in the wine as by-products of fermentation.

First among these is succinic acid, which is the principal cause of the "winey" flavour of wine, its "saveur"; the proportion of succinic acid in a wine, according to Pasteur, is 0.61 per cent of the grape-sugar in the must.

A very small quantity of grape-sugar is also transformed, during fermentation, into acetic acid, proprionic acid and traces of valerianic acid. These acids are present in very small quantities and they do not affect the taste of wine, but they are responsible to a certain extent for its bouquet; the esters, which give the wine its *bouquet*, being formed by alcohols at the expense of acids. Normal wine, that is, wine which is sound and suitably fermented, always contains a little acetic acid, but it is only a very little. When acetic acid is present in wine in a noticeable amount, it is not the result of the decomposition of grape-sugar, but the oxidation of ethyl alcohol; it is a sure sign that the wine is not absolutely sound, that it will soon be vinegar, and no longer wine, if the progress of acetification is not promptly checked.

The variety of volatile and non-volatile acids in wine, which differ from those of the grape-juice, is very great, and Prior's researches have proved that the differences existing in the acids of different wines were due to the differences existing in the species of saccharomycetes and other micro-organisms present in the grape-juice or introduced in the wine at a later date. In every case, those acids are present only in minute quantities, sometimes there are only traces of each, but the importance of the part they play in the degree of excellence of a wine is out of all proportion to their volume.

(d) Aldehydes

Aldehydes are always present in wine. They may be regarded as by-products of alcoholic fermentation and as an intermediary organic compound between alcohols and acids. They must eventually become either acids by the action of oxidising agents, or else alcohols, by the intervention of reducing agents.

(e) Esters

The ethyl formates, acetates, proprionates, butyrates, lactates and other such esters are due to reactions between alcohols and acetic acid, proprionic acid, butyric acid, lactic acid, etc. They are volatile and give to wines their distinctive aroma.

APPENDIX ONE

Vintages and Vintage Charts

We live in the age of the common man, but it does not mean that there are no uncommon men in it – which shows how dangerous all generalizations are bound to be. Vintage charts are certain, by their very nature, to be generalizations and they must, therefore, be used with the full realization that even when a year has been a failure in a certain district, there may be a few, or perhaps only one, lucky *vigneron* who managed to make good wine. It is also, unfortunately, quite possible that when a year is given full marks as a vintage, there may be a few, or perhaps only one, unlucky *vigneron* who made a bad wine.

There follows some notes on vintages, some of very long ago, and a chart of the more recent years prepared by the Wine and Food Society. The notes are mostly for the record and many of the vintages mentioned will not, alas, ever be drunk again, at least not with any pleasure. Such wines *do* exist, some in the private cellars of *propriétaires* like Baron Philippe de Rothschild, at Mouton, or of M. Christian Cruse, at Pontet-Canet; but they are not likely to be opened for us. Here and there in long-forgotten bins a few bottles have kept away their lives, but others may yet live gloriously. May we enjoy the happy accident of meeting them!

The ratings of the following chart range from "o", for a really very bad year, the wines of which are not likely ever to be offered for sale, to "1", a very poor year; "2", also a poor year but with a few exceptions; "3", a year which produced mostly wines from fair to middling in quality; "4" for an irregular year when both quite good and quite indifferent wines were made; "5", a fairly satisfactory year all round; "6", a good vintage which produced mostly fine wines – most of them, however, for early consumption; and "7", when the best vintage conditions obtained and when fine wines were made which should be long-lived and become great with age.

Great Claret Vintages 1840-1929

1841   Very fine quality

1844   Very fine vintage

1846   Fine vintage

There were practically no good vintages in the eighteen-fifties due to the onset of oidium – a fungus disease which ravaged the vineyards for nearly a decade until

1858   'The Comet Year'; a very fine vintage of great lasting power

1864   A splendid vintage

1869   Very fine quality

1870   A very hot summer, with hard but lasting wines, still drinkable and some great today

1871   Some remarkably good wines

1875   Very fine quality

1878   Doubtful at first, but greatly improved with time, the last of the pre-phylloxera wines

No good wines were produced in the 'eighties due to weather, mildew and the devastations of the phylloxera beetles. The early 'nineties were also moderate, although the wines kept well, they were – and are – hard. For twenty years there was no really great wines made on any large scale, but the years

1899 ⎫ produced two of the finest and biggest vintages ever. The wines were
1900 ⎭ big, the nose good and some are still good now (1956)

1917   A good year, but some indifferent wines were made because of the war-time labour shortage

1920   A fine summer and a good vintage

1923   Fine summer and wet autumn; good wines but not of lasting quality

1924   A good vintage

1928   Fine vintage very late in developing. Some wines not ready yet

1929   A very fine vintage indeed; certainly the best since 1900. The wines were full and good from the beginning.

Plate 23 BRANDY. Brandy is distilled from wine; it grows gracious with age if kept in casks but does not improve once bottled. The best glasses for drinking brandy are shown: the medium *ballon*, perfect to savour a wonderful *bouquet*, or the smaller glass which can be held in the palm of one hand, imparting natural warmth, which is very much better than artificially heating the glass before pouring the brandy into it. Larger glasses than these shown are unnecessary and rather ostentatious.

Great Burgundy Vintages 1858-1929

1858 'The Comet Year' – a great year for all French wines
1865 A very fine vintage
1875 A fine vintage with lasting quality
1877 A great vintage
1881
1885
1889 The Burgundian vineyards were not attacked by the phylloxera beetle
1895 until some years after those of Bordeaux. They were able to produce
1898 some excellent wines in the eighties and the nineties
1904 The best were very good
1906 Very good wine of lasting quality
1911 Very good wine of lasting quality
1915 Very fine vintage especially white burgundy
1919 Very good wine indeed but not quite a great year
1923 Light and delicate, but quite superb, by no means weak
1926 A good year
1929 Comparable with 1923, but a bigger wine – a great year

Great Champagne Vintages

Champagne cannot last long; in seven to ten years it is at its best. Fifteen years is a longish life and only in the very best years (like 1921) will the wine remain lively and sparkling for a longer period, although it will be sound enough as 'still' champagne. Consequently the great years are for the record only and only the years are given:

Champagne Vintage Years 1865–1934

1865, 1868, 1874, 1875, 1880, 1884, 1889, 1892, 1893, 1899, 1900, 1904, 1906, 1911, 1920, 1921, 1926, 1928, and 1929.

Plate 24 THE GRAPE WHICH MAKES THE WINE WHICH MAKES THE COGNAC. The *St Emilion*. Not to be confused with the wine of St Emilion (which is made from Merlots and Cabernets), this grape is responsible for the quality of the wine which makes Cognac the supreme spirit. Grown on the chalky soils of the Cognac district, wine made from the St Emilion grape is distilled when very young. Time and patience, skill and experience in blending do the rest.

Year	Bordeaux (Red)	Burgundy (Red)	Rhône	Champagne	Sauternes	Burgundy (White)	Loire	Alsace
1934	6	6	5	6	5	6	5	7
1935	2	4	3	3	2	5	4	5
1936	3	2	5	2	3	4	5	1
1937	5	5	6	5	7	7	7	6
1938	4	3	5	4	3	4	5	4
1939	2	2	3	2	2	2	4	3
1940	3	2	2	3	3	1	3	3
1941	1	1	3	4	0	1	4	2
1942	3	3	5	5	4	4	6	5
1943	5	5	6	5	6	6	7	5
1944	4	2	3	3	4	2	4	3
1945	6	7	6	6	7	6	7	6
1946	3	4	4	3	3	5	6	4
1947	7	7	7	6	7	7	7	6
1948	6	5	4	4	4	5	6	5
1949	7	7	6	5	5	6	5	7
1950	6	4	6	3	4	6	6	5
1951	3	3	4	2	3	3	4	2
1952	7	7	7	7	6	6	7	6
1953	7	7	6	6	7	7	6	7
1954	4	4	5	3	3	4	5	3
1955	6	5	7	7	7	6	7	5
1956	3	2	5	4	4	3	3	2
1957	4	5	4	2	3	5	4	4
1958	5	3	5	3	5	3	5	6

APPENDIX TWO

The Crus Classés du Médoc

The 1855 Classification

Châteaux	Communes	Production (tonneaux)
Premiérs Crus		
Lafite	Pauillac	180
Latour	Pauillac	100
Margaux	Margaux	150
Haut-Brion Graves *	Pessac	100
Deuxièmes Crus		
Mouton-Rothschild	Pauillac	95
Rausan-Ségla	Margaux	60
Rauzan-Gassies	Margaux	50
Léoville-Las-Cases	Saint-Julien	150
Léoville-Poyferré	Saint-Julien	120
Léoville-Barton	Saint-Julien	100
Durfort-Vivens	Margaux	30
Lascombes	Margaux	35
Gruaud-Larose	Saint-Julien	185
Brane-Cantenac	Cantenac	100
Pichon-Longueville	Pauillac	78
Pichon-Longueville-Lalande	Pauillac	100
Ducru-Beaucaillou	Saint-Julien	130
Cos-d'Estournel	Saint-Estèphe	50
Montrose	Saint-Estèphe	100

* Although Château Haut-Brion is in the Commune of Pessac, in the Graves de Bordeaux district, it was included in this classification of Médoc.

151

Châteaux	Communes	Production (tonneaux)
Troisièmes Crus		
Kirwan	Cantenac	100
Issan	Cantenac	30
Lagrange	Saint-Julien	100
Langoa	Saint-Julien	75
Giscours	Labarde	20
Malescot-St. Exupéry	Margaux	50
Cantenac-Brown	Cantenac	90
Palmer	Cantenac	100
La Lagune	Ludon	80
Desmirail	Margaux	30
Calon-Ségur	Saint-Estèphe	150
Ferrière	Margaux	20
d'Alesme-Becker	Margaux	20
Boyd-Cantenac	Cantenac	30
Quatrièmes Crus		
Saint-Pierre-Sevaistre	Saint-Julien	40
Saint-Pierre-Bontemps	Saint-Julien	60
Branaire-Ducru	Saint-Julien	100
Talbot	Saint-Julien	140
Duhart-Milon	Pauillac	140
Pouget	Cantenac	30
La Tour-Carnet	Saint-Laurent	70
Rochet	Saint-Estèphe	60
Beychevelle	Saint-Julien	100
Le Prieuré-Lichine	Cantenac	30
Marquis-de-Terme	Margaux	75
Cinquièmes Crus		
Pontet-Canet	Pauillac	200
Batailley	Pauillac	80
Haut-Batailley	Pauillac	40
Grand-Puy-Lacoste	Pauillac	70

Châteaux	Communes	Production (tonneaux)
Grand-Puy-Ducasse	Pauillac	35
Lynch-Bages	Pauillac	100
Dauzac	Labarde	60
Mouton-Baron-Philippe	Pauillac	100
Le Tertre	Arsac	100
Pédesclaux	Pauillac	30
Belgrave	Saint-Laurent	150
Camensac	Saint-Laurent	70
Cos-Labory	Saint-Estèphe	45
Clerc-Milon-Mondon	Pauillac	35
Croizet-Bages	Pauillac	50
Cantemerle	Macau	100
Lynch-Moussas	Pauillac	Nil
Haut-Bages-Libéral	Pauillac	Nil

An Alphabetical List of Premiers Crus Bourgeois du Médoc

Châteaux	Communes	Average Yield
Abbé-Gorsse-de-Gorsse	Margaux	40
Angludet	Cantenac	60
Anseillan, d'	Pauillac	50
Antonic	Moulis	20
Arche, d'	Ludon	20
Balogue-Haut-Bages	Pauillac	40
Barateau	Saint-Laurent	25
Beaumont	Cussac	100
Beauséjour	Saint-Estèphe	60
Beau-Site	Saint-Estèphe	130
Bellegrave	Pauillac	20
Bellevue	Macau	5

Châteaux	Communes	Average Yield
Bellevue-Cordeillan-Bages	Pauillac	15
Bellevue-Saint-Lambert	Pauillac	40
Biston-Briette	Moulis	20
Bontemps-Dubarry	Saint-Julien	8
Boscq, Le	Saint-Estèphe	70
Bouqueyran	Moulis	40
Canteloup	Saint-Estèphe	80
Capbern	Saint-Estèphe	100
Caronne-Sainte-Gemme	Saint-Laurent	175
Chesnay-Sainte-Gemme, La	Cussac	50
Citran	Avensan	100
Clauzet	Saint-Estèphe	10
Closerie, La	Moulis	38
Conseillant, La	Labarde	40
Corconac	Saint-Laurent	15
Couronne, La	Pauillac	15
Coutelin-Merville (Cru)	Saint-Estèphe	60
Crock, Le	Saint-Estèphe	150
Duplessis-Hauchecorne	Moulis	130
Dutruch-Grand-Poujeaux	Moulis	50
Egmont, d'	Ludon	5
Fatin	Saint-Estèphe	60
Fellonneau	Macau	5
Fonbadet	Pauillac	100
Fonpetite	Saint-Estèphe	130
Fonréaud	Listrac	150
Fontesteau	Saint-Sauveur	50
Fourcas-Dupré	Listrac	50
Fourcas-Hosten	Listrac	70
Grand-Duroc-Milon	Pauillac	15
Gressier-Grand-Poujeaux	Moulis	40
Guitignan	Moulis	25

Châteaux	Communes	Average Yield
Gurgue, La	Margaux	30
Haye, La	Saint-Estèphe	20
Houissant	Saint-Estèphe	80
Labégorce, de	Margaux	100
Lafite-Canteloup	Ludon	20
Lafitte-Carcasset	Saint-Estèphe	60
Lafon	Listrac	30
Lamarque, de	Lamarque	100
Lamothe de Bergeron	Cussac	60
Lamouroux, de	Margaux	20
Lanessan	Cussac	100
Lemoine-Lafon-Rochet	Ludon	15
Lestage	Listrac	180
Lestage-Darquier- Grand-Poujeaux	Moulis	30
Liversan	Saint-Sauveur	70
Ludon-Pomiès-Agassac	Ludon	10
Mac-Carthy	Saint-Estèphe	20
Malescasse	Lamarque	30
Marbuzet, de	Saint-Estèphe	50
Martinens	Cantenac	50
Maucaillou	Moulis	120
Mauvezin	Moulis	20
Meyney	Saint-Estèphe	200
Meyre-Estèbe	Avensan	5
Monbrison	Arsac	40
Montbrun	Cantenac	40
Morère, La	Moulis	20
Morin	Saint-Estèphe	50
Moulin-à-Vent	Moulis	50
Moulis	Moulis	30
Nexon-Lemoyne	Ludon	20
Ormes-de-Pez, Les	Saint-Estèphe	80
Parempuyre, de (Durand-Dassier)	Parempuyre	10
Paveil-de-Luze	Soussans	35
Peyrabon	Saint-Sauveur	200
Pez, de	Saint-Estèphe	100

Châteaux	Communes	Average Yield
Phélan-Ségur	Saint-Estèphe	200
Pibran	Pauillac	30
Picard	Saint-Estèphe	60
Pierre-Bibian	Listrac	70
Pomeys	Moulis	20
Pomys	Saint-Estèphe	25
Pontac-Lynch	Cantenac	15
Poujeaux—Theil	Moulis	180
Ramage-La-Bâtisse (Cru)	Saint-Sauveur	100
Reverdi	Listrac	15
Robert-Franquet	Moulis	25
Roche (Cru)	Saint-Estèphe	40
Romefort	Cussac	20
Rose-Capbern, La	Saint-Estèphe	20
Saint-Estèphe	Saint-Estèphe	30
Saint-Estèphe (Clos)	Saint-Estèphe	25
Saransot-Dupré	Listrac	40
Ségur	Parempuyre	30
Ségur-Fillon (Cru)	Parempuyre	10
Semeillan	Listrac	45
Siran	Labarde	100
Tour-de-Mons, La	Soussans	100
Trois-Moulins, des	Macau	50
Tronquoy-Lalande	Saint-Estèphe	75

An Alphabetical List of the
29 Communes of the Haut-Médoc
with their Potential Production of
Various Grades of Claret
(Red Bordeaux)

Key: A. Wines of the Five Classed Growths *(Crus Classés)*
B. Wines of the *Crus Bourgeois Supérieurs*
C. Wines of the *Crus Bourgeois* and *Crus Artisans*
D. Wines of the *Palus* and *Terrefort* vineyards
E. Totals

Communes	A	B	C	D	E
Arcins	–	–	280	–	280
Arsac	100	32	150	–	282
Avensan	–	155	300	–	455
Blanquefort	–	–	133	300	433
Cantenac	510	205	200	325	1,240
Castelnau	–	–	100	–	100
Cissac	–	–	1,250	–	1,250
Cussac	–	175	500	–	675
Labarde	80	152	65	–	307
Lamarque	–	75	350	–	425
Le Pian-Médoc	–	85	50	–	135
Le Taillan	–	–	400	–	400
Listrac	–	615	1,000	–	1,615
Ludon	20	120	200	600	940
Macau	100	255	200	1,000	1,550
Margaux	140	175	150	210	1,075

Communes	A	B	C	D	E
Moulis	–	830	600	–	1,430
Parempuyre	–	110	–	150	260
Pauillac	1,058	728	1,000	–	2,786
Saint-Aubin	–	–	100	–	100
Saint-Estèphe	505	1,322	1,563	–	3,790
Sainte-Hélène	–	–	20	–	20
Saint-Julien-Beychevelle	1,300	120	250	–	1,670
Saint-Laurent	290	145	500	–	935
Saint-Médard-en-Jalles	–	–	200	–	200
Saint-Sauveur	–	115	250	–	365
Saint-Seurin-de-Cadourne	–	–	1,500	–	1,500
Soussans	–	205	–	250	455
Vertheuil	–	–	1,500	–	1,500
	4,503	6,019	12,821	2,835	26,178

These figures represent *tonneaux* of four *barriques*, roughly speaking 200 gallons or 100 dozen of wine to each *tonneau*.

BIBLIOGRAPHY

A L L E N, H. Warner. The romance of wine. London. 1931.
A contemplation of wine. London. 1951.
Natural red wines. London. 1951.
White wines and Cognac. London. 1952.
Through the wine glass. London. 1954.

A N D R I E U, Pierre. Chronologie anecdotique du vignoble français. Paris. 1944.
Les vins de France et d'ailleurs. Paris. 1939.

B A R R Y, Sir Edward. Observations historical, critical, and medical on the wines
of the Ancients and the analogy between them and modern wines. London.
1775.

B E L L O C, Hilaire. The praise of wine. An heroic Poem. London. 1931.

B E R G E T, Adrien. Les vins de France. Histoire, géographie et statistique du
vignoble français. Paris. 1900.

B E R N E T, Henri. Anthologie des poètes du vin. Lyon. 1944.

B E R R Y, Charles Walter. Viniana. London. 1929.
A miscellany of wine. London. 1932.
In search of wine. A tour of the vineyards of France. London. 1935.

B E R T A L L. La Vigne. Voyage autour des vins de France. Paris. 1878.

B I L L I A R D, Raymond. La vigne dans l'antiquité. Lyon. 1913.

B O I L L O T - D U T H I A U. Notice sur Meursault, son vignoble et la présenta-
tion de ses vins. Meursault. 1947.

B R U N E T, Raymond. Les vins de France. Comment les classer, les vinifier, les
consommer, les présenter. Paris. 1925–1927. 2 vols.
Le vignoble et les vins d'Alsace. Paris. 1932.

BULLIER, Marie. Visages de la Bourgogne. Paris. 1942.

BUREL, Jacques. Le vignoble Beaujolais. Lyon. 1941.

BUTLER, Frank Hedges. Wine and the wine-lands of the world. London. 1926.

CAMPBELL, Ian M. Wayward tendrils of the vine. London. 1948. Reminiscences of a vintner. London. 1950.

CASSAGNAC, Paul de. French wines. Translated by Guy Knowles. London. 1930.

CHALONER, Len. What the vintners sell. London. 1926.

CHAMBERLAIN, Samuel. Bouquet de France. An Epicurean tour of the French Provinces. Illustrated by the author. New York. 1952.

COCKS & FERET. Bordeaux et ses vins classés par ordre de mérite. IIe. édition. Bordeaux. 1949.

DANGUY, M. R. & AUBERTIN, M. Ch. Les grands vins de Bourgogne. Dijon. o.J. (ca. 1892).

DENMAN, James L. The vines and its fruit. London. 1875.

DES OMBIAUX, Maurice. Le Gotha des vins de France. Paris. 1926.

DEWEY, Suzette. Wines: for those who have forgotten, and those who want to know. Chicago. 1934.

ELLIS, Charles. The origin, nature, and history of wine; its use as a beverage lawful and needful to civilized man. London. 1861.

EMERSON, Edward R. Beverages past and present. New York. 1908. 2 vols.

FAES, Henri. Lexique viti-vinicole international: français, italien, espagnol, allemand. Lausanne. 1940.

FOILLARD, Léon & DAVIS, Tony. Le pays et le vin: Beaujolais. Villefranche-en-Beaujolais. 1929.

GALE, Hyman & MARCO, E. Gerald. The How and When: an authoritative Guide to origin, use, and classification of the world's choicest vintages and spirits. Chicago. 1945.

GAY, Charles. Vouvray: ses vignes, ses vignerons. Tours. 1944.

GIRARD, L'Abbé André. La vigne et les vignerons en Sancerrois à travers les siècles. Sancerre. 1941.

GOT, Armand. Les vins doux naturels. Perpignan. 1947.
Monbazillac, hosannah de topaze. Bordeaux. 1949.
La dégustation des vins. Classification des vins. Béziers 1955.

GROSSMANN, Harold. Grossmann's Guide to wines, spirits and beers. New York. 1940. Revised edition, 1953.

HEALY, Maurice. Claret and the white wines of Bordeaux. London. 1934.
Stay me with flagons. London. 1940.
The same, with a running commentary by Ian M. Campbell, and a Memoir by Sir Norman Birkett. London. 1949.

HENDERSON, Al. The history of ancient and modern wines. London. 1824.

LAFORGUE, Germain. Le vignoble girondin. Paris. 1947.

LAVALLE, Dr. Histoire et statistique de la vigne et des grands vins de la Côte d'Or. Paris. 1855.

LICHINE, Alexis. Wines of France. New York, 1951. London. 1952.

LLOYD, F. C. The art and technique of wine. London. 1936.

LOUIS, A. Vignobles et vergers du Midi. Perpignan. 1946.

MAISONNEUVE, Dr. P. Le vigneron angevin. Angers. 1925/6. 2 vols.

MAUMENÉ, E. Traité théorique et pratique du travail des vins. Paris. n.d. 2 vols.

MENDELSOHN, Oscar. The earnest drinker's digest; a short and simple account of alcohol, with a glossary, for curious drinkers. Sydney, 1946. London, 1950.

MEW, James & ASHTON, John. Drinks of the world. London. 1892.

MOWAT, Jean. Anthology of wine. London. 1949.

PASTEUR, Louis. Etudes sur le vin. Paris. 1924.

PELLIGRINI, Angelo. The unprejudiced palate. New York. 1948.

PIC, Albert. Le vignoble de Chablis. Chablis. o.J. (ca. 1934).

POSTGATE, Raymond. The plain man's guide to wine. London. 1951.

POUPON, Pierre & FORGEOT, Pierre. Les vins de Bourgogne. Paris. 1952.

RAMAIN, Dr. Paul. Les grands vins de France. Paris. 1931.

REBOUX, Paul. L'Algérie et ses vins. Algier. 1945.

REDDING, Cyrus. A history and description of modern wines. London. 1833.

ROBSON, E. I. A wayfarer in French vineyards. London. 1928.

RODIER, Camille. Le Clos de Vougeot. Dijon. 1931.
    Le vin de Bourgogne: la Côte d'Or. Dijon, 1937; 1948.

ROGER, J. R. Les vins de Bordeaux. Paris. 1954.

ROUPNEL, Gaston. Le Bourgogne. Paris. 1946.

SAINTSBURY, George. Notes on a cellar book. London. 1920.

SCHOONMAKER, Frank and MARVEL, Tom. The complete wine book.
    New York. 1934; London, 1935.

SCHMITT. Vignes et vins d'Alsace. Colmar. 1949.

SCOTT, J. M. Vineyards of France. Paintings and drawings by Keith Raynes.
    London. 1950.
    The man who made wine. London. 1953.

SHAND, P. Morton. A book of French wines. London. 1928.

SHAW, T. G. Wine, the vine and the cellar. London. 1936.

SHEEN. Wines and other fermented liquors from the earliest ages to the present time. London. 1865.

SIMON, André L. The history of the Champagne trade in England. London. 1905.
The history of the wine trade in England. London. 1906/9. 3 vols.
In vino veritas. London. 1913.
Wine and spirits, the connoisseur's text-book. London. 1919.
The blood of the grape: the wine trade text-book. London. 1920.
Wine and the wine trade. London. 1923.
Bottlescrew Days. London. 1926.
A Dictionary of wine. London. 1935.
Vintagewise. London. 1945.
A wine primer. London. 1946. Revised edition 1956.
Know your wines. London. 1956.
The Wine and Food Menu Book. London. 1956.

STREET, Julian. Wines, their selection, care and service. New York. 1933.
The same, revised by Margot Street. New York. 1948.

THUDICHUM, Dr. J. L. W. & DUPRE, A. A Treatise on the origin, nature, and varieties of wine, being a complete Manual of viticulture and oenology. London. 1872. 2nd. ed. 1896.

TOVEY, Charles. Wine and the wine countries. A record and Manual for wine-merchants and wine consumers. London. 1862.

VIZETELLY, Henry. The wines of the world characterized and classed. London. 1875.

VIZETELLY, Arthur and Ernest. The wines of France. With a chapter on Cognac and table waters. London. (ca. 1908).

GLOSSARY

ACERBE. Sharp. Usually due to immature grapes used in the making of the wine.

AGRAFE. The metal clip used in Champagne to hold the first cork which is replaced when the wine is *dégorge*.

AIGRE. Sour. A wine on the way to the vinegar tub.

ALIGOTE. The second best white grape of Burgundy, the best being the Chardonnay.

AMELIORÉ. Improved. No recommendation; a wine needing improvement was never one of the best.

AMERTUME. Bitterness. Usually a sign that the wine has been kept too long; also a characteristic of wine that is sick from travel and is not yet ready to drink; also a wine that has not yet reached maturity.

APRE. Harsh. A wine which has lost all trace of its original 'fruit'.

ASTRINGENT. Acid; excessively sharp on the palate; usually the wine of a sunless year.

BONDE. Bung.

BOUCHE. Mouth. Vin de Bouche meant 'top table' or best wine in old French.

BOUCHÉ. Corked, in the sense of stoppered with a cork. Vin bouché often means the best wine in the house, in France, where 'ordinaire' is from the cask.

BOUCHONNÉ. Corked, in the sense of corky, a wine from the cask tainted by a defective cork.

BOUQUET. The sweet, clean, pleasing and discreet fragrance which none but the better wines have in their gift.

BRUT. A champagne which has not been sweetened. (In U.S.A. – naturally fermented in the bottle).

CABERNET FRANC. The outstanding black grape of the Médoc; it is grown very extensively in many of the vinelands of the world for the making of fine quality red wines.

CAPITEUX. Heady. A wine usually of high alcoholic strength.

CAPSULE. Metal cap protecting the outside face of the cork from damp mould and insects.

CAQUE. Osier basket used for carrying the picked ripe grapes from vineyard to press at the vintage time.

CELLIER. Wine-vault or store

CEP. Vine stock.

CÉPAGE. Species of vine; it is to different cépages that grapes owe their colour and flavour.

CHAI. An above ground storage place for wine in casks, as distinct from the cellar which is below ground.

CHAMBRER. To allow red wine gradually to acquire room temperature.

CHAPTALISER. The adding of sugar to the grapes when being crushed at vintage time in order to obtain a higher alcoholic degree than the wine would acquire through the fermentation of its own grape-sugar.

CHARNU. Fleshy, in the sense of a red wine with fat body.

CHÂTEAU. Homestead, whether castle or cottage, of a wine producing Estate. 'Mise en bouteille au Château' or 'Mise du Château' means that the wine was bottled where it was made. It is a birth certificate but not necessarily a certificate of merit.

CHENIN BLANC. A white grape species grown mostly in the Loire valley for the making of quality white wine.

CLIMAT. The name given in Burgundy to certain vineyards; it means a 'growth' or *cru*.

COLLER. To fine, or clarify, a new or young wine in the barrel before racking or bottling it.

CORPS. Stout. A wine with full body.

CORSÉ. Well-built. A wine with rather bigger body and a greater alcoholic strength than most, but well balanced withal.

COUPÉ. Cut, in the sense of a wine blended with another.

COULANT. Easy to drink, in the sense of a simple, light, pleasing wine, the first glass of which is not to be the last.

CRÉMANT. Creaming, or slightly sparkling; crackling.

CRU. A named vineyard, or range of vineyards producing wines of the same quality and standard.

CUVE. Vat.

CUVÉE. Vatting. The wine made from a blend of wines of the same vintage but of different vineyards; or of different vintages of the same wine; it usually bears a name or a number for the sake of identification until it is all sold or drunk, when another Cuvée is offered.

In Champagne, the wine made from the first pressings of the grapes is the best, and is known as *Vin de Cuvée*.

DÉGORGER. Removing the sediment from a bottle of Champagne by drawing the first cork with very little loss of wine and gas.

DEMI-SEC. Rather sweet Champagne, not 'half-dry'.

DEPÔT. Sediment.

DOUX. Sweet.

DUR. Hard. A wine with an excess of tannin.

EGRAPPÉES. Grapes which have been freed from their stalks.

EGRAPPOIR. A rotating callender-barrel used for freeing grapes from the stalks.

ELÉGANT. A delicate, slight but attractive wine.

FAIBLE. Weak.

FERME. Rather hard but not unpleasantly so.

FEUILLETTE. Half hogshead.

FINIT BIEN. A wine with a particularly pleasing 'farewell' or smooth 'finish'.

FOUDRES. Vats of large capacity used for blending wines.

FRANC DE GOÛT. Straightforward and intensely 'clean' on the palate.

FRAPPÉ. Iced.

FRUITÉ. Fruity, in the sense of a wine which has retained some of its original grape sugar.

GAMAY. One of the most extensively cultivated red wine grapes, which produces more but commoner wine than the Pinot, although in the Maconnais, Chalonnais and Beaujolais it is responsible for quite fair red wines.

GAZÉIFIÉ. A sparkling wine with carbonic acid gas pumped into it.

GÉNÉREUX. A fortified wine, usually sweet and spirity.

GOÛT. Taste.

GOÛT AMÉRICAIN. A fairly sweet wine, chiefly Champagne.

GOÛT ANGLAIS. A dry wine, chiefly Champagne.

GOÛT DE BOIS. A wine which tastes of the wood of the cask, a defect due to a faulty stave or too long a stay in the cask.

GOÛT DE BOUCHON. A wine tainted by a defective cork.

GOÛT D'EVENT. A wine which tastes flat, usually when left open too long.

GOÛT FRANÇAIS. A sweet Champagne.

GOÛT DE PAILLE. A wine with an objectionable taste of wet straw.

GOÛT DE PIERRE À FUSIL. A wine with a not objectionable 'flint' taste.

GOÛT DE PIQUÉ. A wine with an objectionable vinegary taste.

GOÛT DE POURRI. A wine with an objectionable mouldy taste.

GOÛT DE RANCIO. A wine with a slightly rancio taste due to very old age when it becomes very sweet and resembles Madeira. Some people like it, others do not.

GOÛT DE TERROIR. A wine with a distinctively earthy taste peculiar to the soil of its vineyard.

GROSSIER. Common or coarse.

HECTARE. A land measure equal to 2.47 acres.

HECTOLITRE. A liquid measure equal to 26.4178 American gallons or 22 English gallons.

LIQUEUR DE TIRAGE. Sugar candy melted in champagne wine and added to Champagne at the time of bottling.

LIQUOREUX. A particularly sweet, fortified wine.

MADÉRISÉ. A wine with a slight taste of rancio. It becomes sweeter in ageing and resembles Madeira.

MARC. The stalks, pips and skins which are left after the grape-juice has been pressed out of the grapes. If sugar and water are added to the Marc, it ferments and the poor wine made from it is called Piquette; when distilled it is called Eau-de-vie de Marc. It is distilled usually at a very high strength and needs years of storage to become mellow and acceptable.

MERLOT. One of the important species of black grapes responsible for the excellence of the red wines of Bordeaux.

MILLÉSIME. The date of the vintage.

MILLÉSIMÉ. A 'dated' or vintage wine.

MOELLEUX. Soft and smooth.

MOU. Flabby, unattractive wine.

MOUILLÉ. Watered.

MOUSSEUX. Sparkling.

MOÛT. Unfermented grape juice or must.

MÛR. Ripe.

MUTÉ. A wine the fermentation of which has been arrested by the addition of spirit to the grape-juice.

NATURE. A still or sparkling Champagne which has not been 'sweetened'.

NERVEUX. A wine with every promise of keeping long and improving with age.

NU. Bare. The price of the wine without the cost of cask or bottles.

OEIL DE PERDRIX. The colour of 'onion skin'. A tawny *Vin Rosé*.

ORDINAIRE. Plain or undistinguished wine.

PASSE-TOUS-GRAINS. A red wine in Burgundy from both Pinot and Gamay grapes.

PASTEURISÉ. Pasteurized, a wine treated by heat to kill all ferments.

PAYS, Vin De. Local wine, usually *ordinaire*.

PAYSAN, Vin De. Peasant wine, usually *très ordinaire*.

PELURE D'OIGNON. Onion skin colour, pale tawny. A *Vin Rosé*.

PÉTILLANT. Crackling, slightly sparkling.

PIÈCE. Hogshead, holds about 225 litres.

PINOT BLANC or CHARDONNAY. A white grape grown in Burgundy and Champagne for fine quality wines.

PINOT NOIR or NOIRIEN. A black grape grown in Burgundy and Champagne for fine quality wines.

PIQUÉ. Pricked. A wine on the way to the vinegar tub.

PIQUETTE. An imitation wine made from the pressed-out husks of grapes, which are flooded with water, sweetened with the cheapest available sugar and fermented with brewer's yeast. A poor, watery and sharp wine.

PLAT. Flat. A dull and flat wine that will never be better and is not worth keeping.

PLÂTRÉ. Plastered, that is with gypsum or some sort of lime added to clarify the wine.

POURRITURE NOBLE. A form of mould which settles on Sauvignon, Semillon, and Riesling grapes, known as 'botrytis cinerea'; it is responsible for the sweetness of Sauternes and Palatinate wines.

PRÉCOCE. Forward. A wine that is maturing uncommonly rapidly.

PRESSOIR. Apparatus used for pressing the grapes.

QUARTAUT. A small barrel containing about 56 litres.

QUEUE. The name given to a couple of hogsheads in Burgundy; many wines are sold by the queue, i.e. by two hogsheads.

RACE. Breed.

ROBE. The wine's colour.

ROSÉ. There are *Vins Rosés*, light red wines, made practically everywhere where black grapes grow, chiefly still or table wines in the Gironde and Burgundy, but also sparkling wines in Champagne and the Loire Valley. The majority of still *Vins Rosés* are made of black grapes which are pressed in the Champagne fashion, that is with their juice being fermented away from the black skins which hold the red pigment responsible for the colour of all red wines. When the separation of juice and skins is done in a more leisurely manner than is the practice in Champagne, it gives the juice a chance to be dyed pink. This easiest of all methods to make *Vins Rosés* is best for all the cheaper types of wine, that is wines which are intended for quick consumption, but it is not so good for wines like Champagne, which may not be drunk until a few years old, as the pink may either fade or become brownish. A much more lasting pink 'dye' is that which is obtained from cochineal: it is absolutely tasteless and has no smell of any sort, so that it may safely be used to colour white wines pink when fashion demands *Vins Rosés*.

SAINT-EMILION. This wine is deeper in colour than most Médoc wines, but it does not last so long and seldom possesses as refined a *bouquet* as the Graves.

SAUVIGNON BLANC. One of the finest species of white grapes. Used for fine white wines such as Pouilly-Fumé and when mixed with Semillon grapes excellent Sauternes wines are produced.

SEC. Dry, when speaking of table wines. A 'sec' Champagne is sweet, but when 'demi-sec' it is sweeter; 'extra-sec' means dry.

SEMILLON. A species of white grapes which, together with Sauvignon, is responsible for all the best white wines of Bordeaux and many other vineyards.

SÈVE. As the sap is life to the vine, so is Sève to the wine; it means a well-balanced, well-knit wine with the prospect of a long life.

SOUCHE. Root stock.

SOUTIRAGE. Racking.

SOYEUX. Silky, smooth, most attractive wine, free from all traces of tannin or acidity.

SYLVANER. One of the white grapes grown on a large scale in Alsace, Germany and Austria for the making of fair quality white wines.

SYRAH. One of the black grapes chiefly grown in the Rhône valley, more particularly at Hermitage, for the making of quality red table wines.

TENDRE. Tender, in the sense of light and pleasing, but not likely to be a particularly lasting wine.

TÊTE DE CUVÉE. First drawing off of the wine which is made from pickings of chosen, over-ripe grapes, in the Sauternes district. In Burgundy the Têtes de Cuvée are the best wines, red or white, from any particular vineyard.

TIRAGE. Bottling. Wines, red or white, from any particular vineyard.

TIRAGE D'ORIGINE. Original bottling, this is used in Burgundy where some shippers decant wines of any age before sending them to merchants or consumers, free from all lees.

TONNEAU. A Bordeaux wine measure equal to 4 hogsheads.

USÉ. Worn. A wine that has been kept too long.

VELOURS. Velvet. A somewhat full and particularly soft wine.

VENDANGE. Gathering of the grapes – the grape harvest.

VIN DOUX NATUREL. Unfortified, sweet dessert wine with a minimum alcoholic strength of 14°.

VIGNERON. Vine grower.

INDEX

[1] These are indexed under the first capital letter; thus, 'La Closerie' will be found under 'L', but 'de l'Angelus' under 'A'.

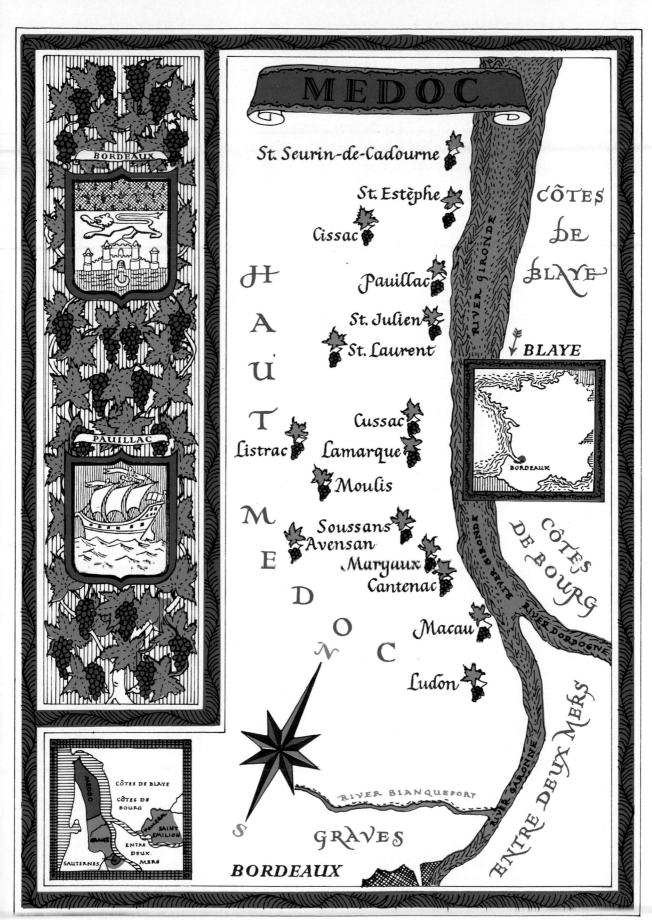

MEDOC

St. Seurin-de-Cadourne
St. Estèphe
Cissac
Pauillac
St. Julien
St. Laurent

CÔTES DE BLAYE

River Gironde

BLAYE

Cussac
Listrac
Lamarque
Moulis
Soussans
Avensan
Maryaux
Cantenac

CÔTES DE BOURG

River Dordogne

Macau

Ludon

HAUT MEDOC

N

S

River Blanquefort

GRAVES

BORDEAUX

River Garonne

ENTRE DEUX MERS

BORDEAUX

PAUILLAC

MEDOC
CÔTES DE BLAYE
CÔTES DE BOURG
GRAVES
SAINT EMILION
ENTRE DEUX MERS
SAUTERNES

MAP I

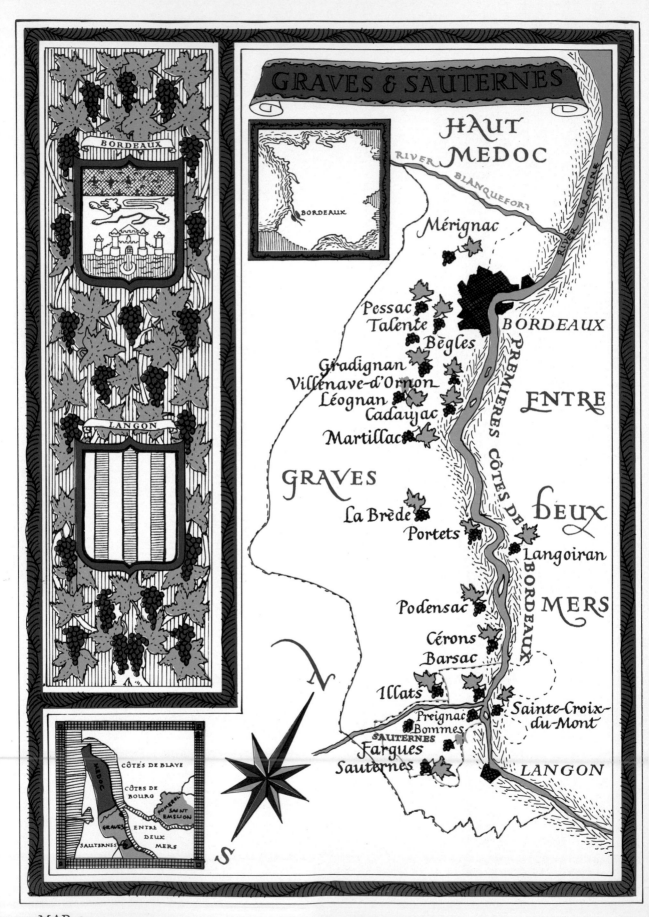

GRAVES & SAUTERNES

HAUT MEDOC

RIVER BLANQUEFORT

RIVER GARONNE

Mérignac

Pessac
Talente
Bègles
Gradignan
Villenave-d'Ornon
Léognan
Cadaujac
Martillac

BORDEAUX

GRAVES

La Brède
Portets

Langoiran

Podensac

Cérons
Barsac

Illats

Preignac
Bommes
SAUTERNES
Fargues
Sauternes

Sainte-Croix-du-Mont

LANGON

PREMIERES CÔTES DE BORDEAUX

ENTRE

DEUX

MERS

BORDEAUX

BORDEAUX

LANGON

CÔTES DE BLAYE
CÔTES DE BOURG
MEDOC
POMEROL
SAINT EMILION
GRAVES
ENTRE DEUX MERS
SAUTERNES

MAP 2

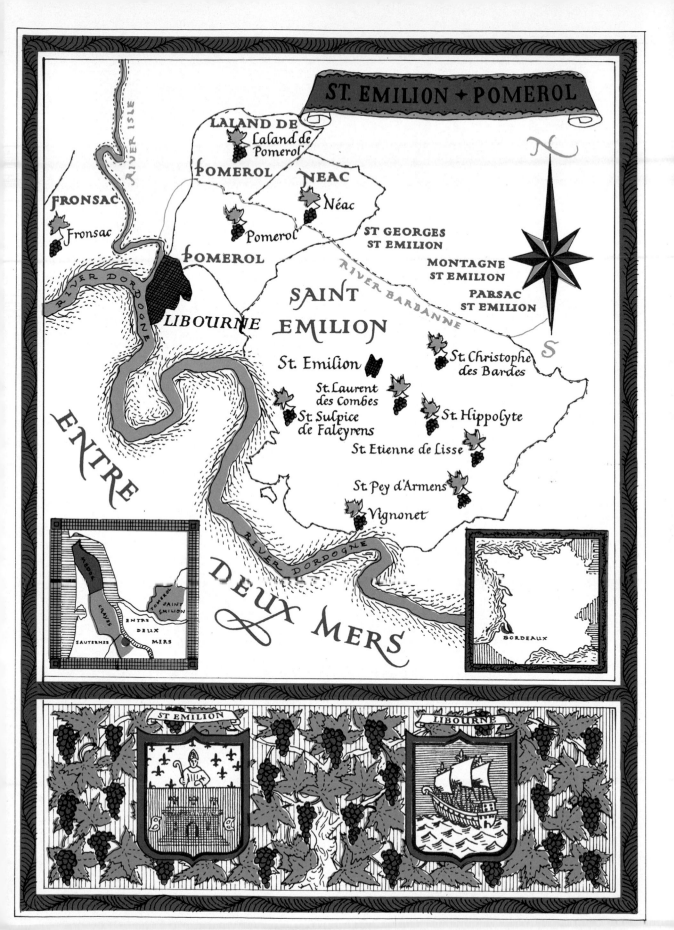

ST. EMILION ✦ POMEROL

LALAND DE
Laland de
Pomerol

POMEROL

NEAC
Néac

FRONSAC
Fronsac

POMEROL
Pomerol

ST GEORGES
ST EMILION

POMEROL
LIBOURNE

MONTAGNE
ST EMILION

PARSAC
ST EMILION

RIVER BARBANNE

SAINT
EMILION

St. Emilion

St Christophe
des Bardes

St. Laurent
des Combes

St Sulpice
de Faleyrens

St. Hippolyte

St Etienne de Lisse

St Pey d'Armens

Vignonet

RIVER ISLE

RIVER DORDOGNE

ENTRE

DEUX MERS

RIVER DORDOGNE

MEDOC

GRAVES

POMEROL
SAINT
EMILION

ENTRE
DEUX
MERS

SAUTERNES

BORDEAUX

ST EMILION

LIBOURNE

MAP 3

BOURGOGNE

NUITS

BURGUNDY

DIJON ■

Fixin

Gevrey-Chambertin

Chambolle-Musigny

Morey St Denis

Vougeot

Flagey-
Echezeaux

Vosne-Romanée

CÔTE DE NUITS

Nuits
St. Georges

Prémeaux

Savigny
les-Beaune

Aloxe Corton

Beaune

CÔTE DE BEAUNE

Auxey-
Duresses

Pommard

Volnay
Monthelie
Meursault

Nolay

Blagny

Puligny-Montrachet

Chassagne-
Montrachet

Santenay

Rully

CÔTE

Mercurey

Givry

CHALON ■

CHALONNAISE

Montagny

RIVER SAONE

Cluny

Lugny

TOURNUS ■

Viré

MACONNAIS

N

Fuisse

Pouilly-Loche

Vinzelles

Mâcon ■

St. Amour

Julienas

S

Chenas-Moulin-a-Vent

Fleurie

Chiroubles

Morgon

Côte de
Brouilly

Brouilly

RIVER SAONE

BEAUJOLAIS

TO LYONS

CHABLIS

Blanchot
Les Clos
Grenouille
Preuze
Valmur
Vaudésir

Bougros
Chapelots
Fourchaume
Mont de Milieu
Montée de Tonnerre
Vaulorent

DIJON

LYONS

MAP 4

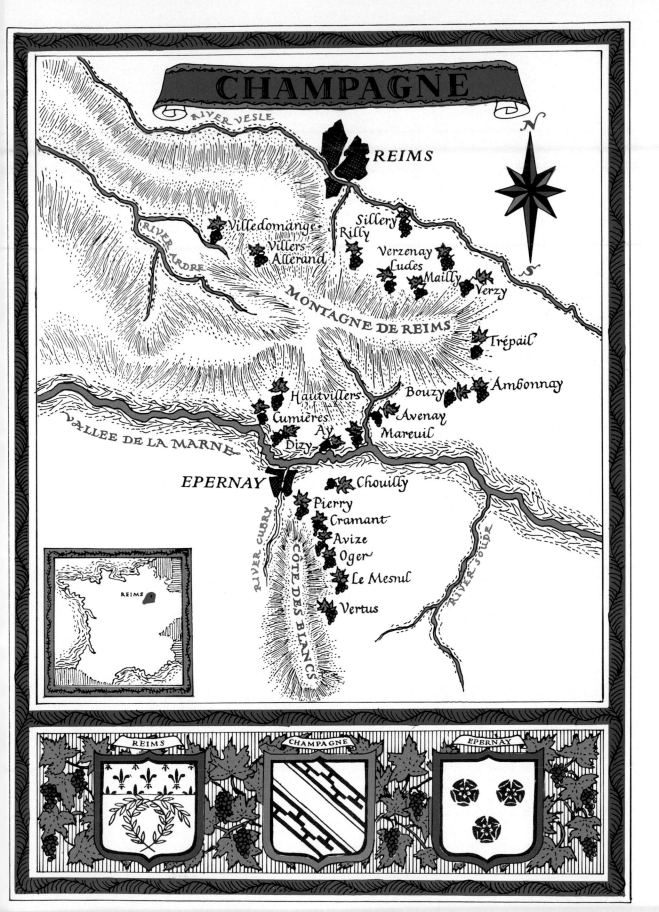

CHAMPAGNE

RIVER VESLE

REIMS

N

S

Villedomange

Sillery

Rilly

Villers

Allerand

Verzenay

Ludes

Mailly

Verzy

RIVER ARDRE

MONTAGNE DE REIMS

Trépail

Ambonnay

Hautvillers

Bouzy

Cumières

Avenay

Ay

Mareuil

VALLEE DE LA MARNE

Dizy

EPERNAY

Chouilly

Pierry

Cramant

Avize

Oger

Le Mesnil

RIVER CUBRY

CÔTE DES BLANCS

RIVER SOUDE

REIMS

Vertus

REIMS

CHAMPAGNE

EPERNAY

MAP 5

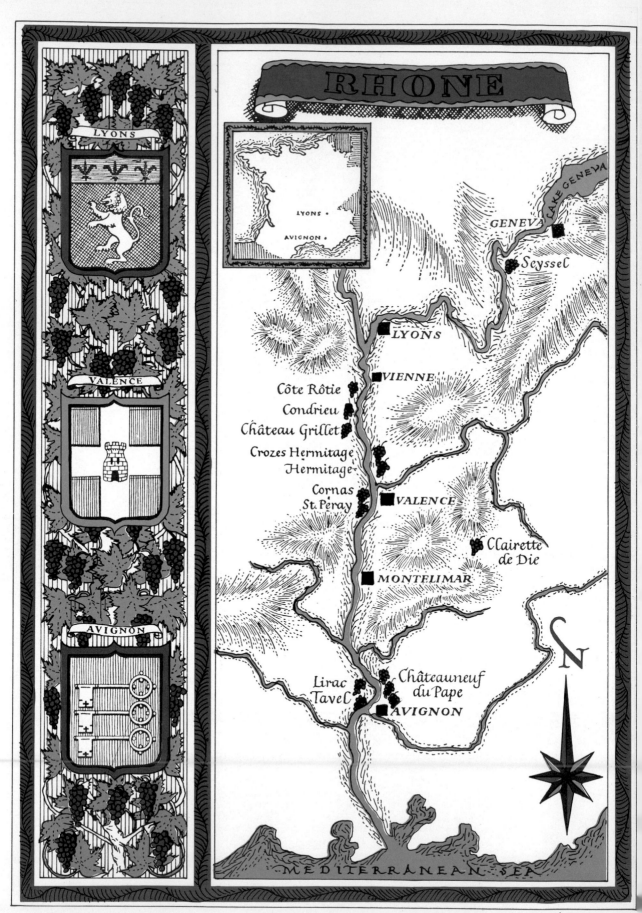

RHONE

LYONS

VALENCE

AVIGNON

LAKE GENEVA

LYONS •

AVIGNON •

GENEVA

Seyssel

LYONS

VIENNE

Côte Rôtie
Condrieu
Château Grillet
Crozes Hermitage
Hermitage
Cornas
St. Peray

VALENCE

Clairette
de Die

MONTELIMAR

Lirac
Tavel

Châteauneuf
du Pape

AVIGNON

N

MEDITERRANEAN SEA

MAP 6

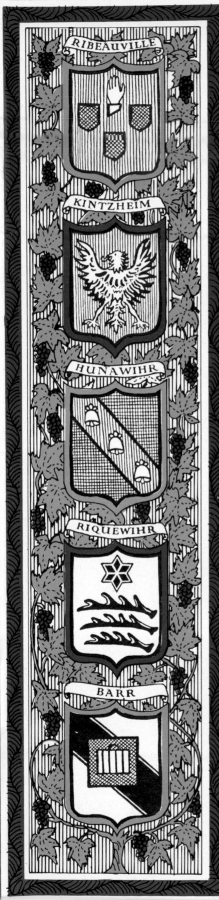

RIBEAUVILLE

KINTZHEIM

HUNAWIHR

RIQUEWIHR

BARR

ALSACE

STRASBOURG

Wolheim

Molsheim

Obernai

Barr

Mittelbergheim

Dambach

SÉLESTAT

Kintzheim

Bergheim

Ribeauville

Hunawihr

Riquewihr

Mittelwihr

Ammerschwihr

Kaysersberg

COLMAR

Wintzenheim

Eguisheim

Guebwiller

Thann

MULHOUSE

VOSGES

BAS-RHIN

HAUT-RHIN

RIVER ILL

RIVER RHINE

RIVER RHINE

RIVER ILL

STRASBOURG
COLMAR
MULHOUSE

MAP 7

COGNAC

LA ROCHELLE

BONS BOIS

Saint Jean d'Angély

FINS BOIS

BOIS A TERROIR

ORDINAIRES

PETITE CHAMPAGNE

ÎLE D'OLÉRON

RIVER CHARENTE

Jarnac

Cognac

Saintes

Angoulême

GRAND CHAMPAGNE

Ségonzac

BONS BOIS

Archiac

BOIS

FINS BOIS

Barbézieux

PETITE CHAMPAGNE

RIVER NE

ATLANTIC OCEAN

RIVER GIRONDE

FINS BOIS

LA ROCHELLE

COGNAC

ANGOULEME

MAP 8